The Underground Heart

The Under

ground Heart

A Return to a Hidden Landscape

essays by **Ray Gonzalez**

The University of Arizona Press   TUCSON

The University of Arizona Press

♾ This book is printed on acid-free, archival-quality paper.
Manufactured in the United States of America

07 06 05 04 03 02   6 5 4 3 2 1

Library of Congress Cataloging-in-Publication Data

Gonzalez, Ray.
The underground heart : a return to a hidden landscape : essays / by Ray Gonzalez.
p. cm. — (Camino del sol)
ISBN 0-8165-2032-1 (acid-free paper) —
ISBN 0-8165-2034-8 (pbk. : acid-free paper)
1. Gonzalez, Ray—Homes and haunts—Texas. 2. Gonzalez, Ray—Homes and haunts—New
Mexico. 3. Authors, American—20th century—Biography. 4. Southwestern States—Social
conditions. 5. Mexican American authors—Biography. 6. New Mexico—Social conditions.
7. Texas—Social conditions. 8. Mexican American families. I. Title. II. Series.
PS3557.0476 Z478 2002
814'.54—dc21   2002001850

British Library Cataloguing-in-Publication Data
A catalogue record for this book is available from the British Library.

Publication of this book is made possible in part by the proceeds of a permanent endowment
created with the assistance of a Challenge Grant from the National Endowment for the Humanities,
a federal agency.

Contents

The Underground Heart: A Return to a Hidden Landscape is a book about coming home, returning to the desert Southwest as a native son who has lived in other parts of the country for more than twenty years. It is a book about driving through the Southwest, playing tourist, and seeing historical sights (heritage tourism is one of the key themes in these essays). Having been gone for more than two decades, I returned to an El Paso area that does not look the same as the one in which I grew up; it has been developed and transformed into a place people from other parts of the country should want to visit. Tourist bureaus are doing their job of selling a historically impoverished area to visitors who know nothing about the Southwest. *The Underground Heart* goes behind the slogans (Land of Enchantment, the Lone Star State) and the latest Mexican food craze to uncover a deeper place. The rejuvenation of border culture, fueled by tourist and trade dollars, may be surprising to readers who hear only the gritty news stories about illegal immigration, the NAFTA agreement, and the ongoing political clashes between the United States and Mexico, two nations with people trying to live in one country.

These essays go beyond my childhood years to show how my early romantic notions about deserts and mountains have changed to reflect a more sobering way of life along the U.S.–Mexican border. It is not enough to say there are more strip malls, freeways, and suburbs in the Chihuahuan Desert of west Texas and southern New Mexico. As a native of the area, I had to go back and rediscover the land of my past to understand the hyper, bilingual atmosphere of its future. The desert, the Rio Grande, and the Franklin Mountains may have made me a poet, as my grandmother's stories bound my family's past together, but the barbed wire, buried sensors, and Border Patrol vans of today have turned poetic license into a note of inquiry, searching, and loss. The hidden landscapes of anyone's home can be revealed only when true compassion and understanding follow objective distance, then intense submersion into a place that allowed the dweller to leave long ago. The underground heart of home beats as I drive the highways of New Mexico and west Texas, my car lost among thousands of vehicles lining up to cross international bridges, their tires of heat and curiosity running over antiquated boundary lines that were erased by history long ago.

Acknowledgments

Thanks to the editors of the following publications where some of these essays first appeared:

Crab Orchard Review, parts of "The Return"
National Public Radio's National Park Project, "The Underground Heart"
Roundup: An Anthology of Texas Poets, parts of "The Border Is Open"
The Color of Nature: Multicultural Essays on the Environment (Milkweed Editions), "Hazardous Cargo"
Turnrow, "The Death of the Poet"

Urban Nature: An Anthology (Milkweed Editions), parts of "Tortas Locas" *Creative Non-Fiction,* "The General on the Border"

I would like to thank the University of Minnesota, Twin Cities, for a McKnight Land Grant Fellowship and a President's Research Grant that gave me time to travel and do research in the southwestern United States. A special thanks goes to the Pikes Peak Writers Retreat, the Corporation of Yaddo, and the Loft Studio Program for time and valuable space in which to work on these essays. For their skills in leading me in the right direction, I thank the staffs of the El Paso Public Library, the Albuquerque Public Library, the University of New Mexico Library, and the University of Texas at El Paso Library and Rare Book Archives. In addition, the curators at the Albuquerque History Museum, the Museum of Santa Fe, and at Hueco Tanks State Park offered their valuable time and knowledge when I visited. This book could not have been written without the support and patience of Patti Hartmann at the University of Arizona Press. My deepest thanks and respect for her work. During my year away from teaching, many friends and family provided shelter, inspiration, and ideas. The long list of generous people includes Ida Steven, Beatrice Gonzalez, Phil Woods, Juan Felipe Herrera, Morton Marcus, Virgil Suarez, Tom and Marilyn Auer, Maria Tabor, and Rafael Jesus Gonzalez. Special gratitude goes to my research assistant, Michelle Matthees, for her two and a half years of hard, detailed work.

Part One

The Return

I drive over Raton Pass, the scenic mountain route into northern New Mexico from Colorado, and spot the black clouds in the valley below. My road weariness quickly disappears when the first lightning bolt hits the trees east of the highway. I am alert as it starts to rain heavily, the breaking thunder and lightning appearing at seven thousand feet. On the tape deck, "The Allman Brothers Band: The Fillmore Concerts," one of my favorite albums of all time, has kept me company through Colorado. The instant the lightning bolts punch the mountains, the Allmans launch into an incredible version of "In Memory of Elizabeth Reed," the instrumental with some of Duane Allman's and Dickey Betts' finest guitar work. They play the right song at the right time because I never planned for this—huge thunder rolls shaking the car and walls of water obscuring the road ahead. I wish for a gas station, but there is no place to stop on the high pass and the storm is right over me, the band playing faster as my car weaves through the storm from the skies and the one vibrating the car speakers.

The speed of the song and the pounding rain make me increase my speed on the slick highway as it begins its curving descent into New Mexico. Giant pines and broken boulders along the highway flash by when I pass a lumber truck on its left. I am getting very nervous; the music sounds different and more intense, matching my fear. The dark rain becomes deafening as Duane goes into his first solo, his guitar hands rising through ghost images of past concerts and young guitarists flying away in the prime of their young careers. My windshield wipers, squeaking on fast speed, can't clear the windshield fast enough or keep up with Duane's biting notes. Another truck ahead of me sprays the air with water and makes it hard for me to see the road. The instrumental song, supposedly about a woman Dickey seduced on a tombstone in Georgia, slows down and relaxes before the last section in which Duane and Betts trade slashing note after note. This is unexpected energy from a classic rock band, and their falling guitars and lightning bolts, plus the sheer magnificence of the mountains, have me flying down the dangerous pass at increasing speeds.

Two more lightning bolts hit on the other side of the highway with reverberating thunder. I have enjoyed the sight of distant storms across the desert as their faraway lightning entered the earth without a sound, but I have never seen so many strikes near a major road. This time I am right in it, shooting down a risky highway where Colorado is saying good-bye, New Mexico is welcoming me with black rain clouds in magnetic fields, and the Allman Brothers are in heart-attack mode. No one knows I am returning to New Mexico for the first time in years, and I feel like a stranger, but the Allmans and the lightning grab my teen-age ghosts and hurl them against my vibrating car. I want to feel like I've never been gone and that my favorite musicians who guided me through the desert never died.

My heart wants to explode from the weather and the music, but I don't give in; I grip the wheel tighter, shooting curve after curve. As I descend, the pine-covered hills turn purple to match the music inside the car. Four lightning bolts hit miles south of the pass and the purple mountains flash a brilliant white. Despite the rain against the windshield, I can see the mountains getting closer as Duane steps aside and Dickey begins his fiery shots. Every few seconds, I trade moments of memorable songs with flashes of a country I have not enjoyed in a long time. Waves of icy water force me to turn on the defroster as the team of drummers on the tape pushes me to switch lanes.

It starts to hail when I come out of the pass and enter New Mexico, so I turn up the volume on the cassette and begin to shake in my seat. The hail hammers the rental car and I can't see ten yards ahead of me. A number of cars, even large trucks, have pulled over to the shoulder of the road to wait for the hailstorm to pass. The highway is covered in white as if a blizzard just passed. I take a big gulp from my bottle of water, the first chance I have had to drink for miles. My fingers and palms hurt from gripping the steering wheel.

I am tempted to turn the volume down and stop, but the Allmans keep me from pulling over. Just as Duane on his motorcycle didn't stop in 1971, I don't want to stop. Duane never came back. I don't want to sit in my car at the side of the road and turn deaf from the shattering hail, choosing instead to ruin my hearing from an orgiastically loud playing of "Whipping Post," the most savage song on the tape and one I am glad did not make its appearance during the accelerating descent down Raton. If I had experienced the timeless moments on "Whipping Post" high up on the pass, my car might have gone off the mountain. It sounds ridiculous, but meeting my favorite rock band from the past, thousands of feet above New Mexico, is an out-of-body experience that die-hard rock fans can understand. How many of us get to face our ancient, electric demons atop peaks attacked by lightning? Another bolt hits a few miles to the west as I try to catch my breath.

Slowing down, I drive through the hail at twenty-five miles an hour. The pieces of ice were huge and I thought they would crack the windshield, but as I weave through the downpour, the white pellets grow smaller and smaller. At last I have descended from Raton Pass, and I am driving onto the level plains of northeastern New Mexico, monitoring the length of the hailstorm on the mileage meter. There are seven miles of hail before it finally stops.

On the last stretch of ice, the back wheels of the car slide for a couple of seconds, then grip the road. I place my right hand momentarily on the briefcase that rests on the passenger seat. Inside, among notebooks and papers, I carry my contributor's copy of a literary journal that recently published my prose poem about the one time I saw the original Allman Brothers Band play. I brought it with me because it came in the stack of mail that arrived just before this trip. Among recent publications, it is the one I have anticipated for months, and I think about the piece when I calm down and get through the bad weather.

I have not had time to memorize these lines under the heading "The Allman Brothers Band: The Fillmore Concerts":

The greatest live album of all time—so magnetic and dangerous, I go through periods of being afraid to play it. I saw the Allman Brothers in concert two weeks before Duane died. Las Cruces, 1971. Stoned and trying to stay in the space between the red sunset and the asphalt highway that ran for miles and miles through the desert, trying to get to the arena in the Mesilla Valley. Dickey Betts' solo on "Whipping Post" the most damaging and monumental guitar solo since the damned instrument was invented. No one knows this but me. It is there on the record. I have written several hundred poems off this recording, twisted my writing life around this album. No one knows this but me. Black cover on the original, vinyl LP. The remastered CD perhaps the one with the best sound I have heard from the new technology. The biggest shock on the new version is the fact they cut the infamous shout from the audience right before the band starts to play the long song. The dude used to shout, "Whipping Post!" from the crowd and Duane would answer, "You got it!" then Berry Oakley's bass would start pounding as the band pulled your heart out with its seventeen-minute fury—this moment erased on the CD version! The highway between El Paso and Las Cruces gone on this version. The image of Gregg sitting at his organ and Duane and Dickey eating their burning fingers gone from this version. Duane's death gone from this version.

The Allmans play and I keep going. The hail has ended and light rain falls for another half hour. I pick up speed when the white on the road turns to black, wet asphalt again. I have entered New Mexico with lightning and thunder, flown down the pass with the Allman Brothers, who have destroyed the peaceful air of the Southwest in a manner more lethal than lightning—a tape I put in the car's player way back in Pueblo, Colorado, one hundred miles ago. By this time, Gregg Allman is singing, "Cause there's a man down there! Must be your man, I don't know!" His growling voice is the ghost of performing men and those who have flown down the highway behind me, electric sounds from personal archives and from the angry sky that resists welcoming me back as I bounce over the peaks, descending through forests that don't care. These mountains and valleys of northern New Mexico don't care because their magical stage made room for an electric wind of guitars and rain long ago.

The Border Is Open

Home is where our individual memories are rooted and never disappear, the place where our inner being begins and ends, a haven for birth and death. Home is the place where we return when we need to adjust to new energies the world presses upon our daily lives. Home is comfort and uneasiness. Despite the age-old cliché of not being able to go home again, we carry home wherever we dwell. If we never leave our hometown to live elsewhere, which is true for a large percentage of the American population, we create our territory of existence in the place where we were born—home. The character of that home is vastly different from the one created elsewhere by people who left their hometown ages ago. Home as territory—fortress or open house.

As a native of the Southwest, I know my home will always be the desert surrounding El Paso and the southern New Mexico area. I left in 1979 but have never been able to create a natural sense of home in other cities where I have lived. The memory of the desert creates an invisible nest of roots that allows a native to wander far before finding a way back. The memory of the Rio Grande passing its vein of mud south is one I sleep with, then wake to see if the level of the current has gone down. The stark peaks of the Franklin Mountains dominate the city that grows in a horseshoe shape around them. El Paso spreads for miles into the desert east of the mountains. Housing developments tear high into the Franklins themselves. The horseshoe is now bent and twisted, its boundaries of my childhood gone. I gaze up at the bare face of the Franklins and conclude that the crown of my home has eroded over the forty-nine years of my life. Each time I come home, the mountains are closer to the ground.

Memories of wandering the desert alone as a boy and teaching myself about the rocks, the fossils stuck inside them, and the tarantulas scuttling across my dirt path pull me back home. Childhood memories that made me leave rise when I visit my home—the silent father, the boys who chased me off the football team, the grandmother who always wanted me by her side. The happy experiences—the climb up muddy arroyos after a desert rain, riding tiny paddleboats at the amusement park on the other side of town— have me wishing I could go back in time. Home is the generator of longing. It is the yearning for a united family, happy Christmas days, innocent adventures with the kids next door. It is also the place where the person we wanted to be when we grew up never appeared, because we became someone else. The great Catholic fear during Sunday mass and the racism in high school stand out in my mind. Later, it was my divorced parents and my dreams of being successful in careers that never materialized, until I accomplished many things I never thought I would. Home created a different individual because El Paso educated my heart and mind, placing its limits upon me. Such limits often match the city limits of our hometown as we grow up, so we are forced to go live elsewhere.

I visualize rattlesnakes, lizards, bats, turtles, scorpions, hawks, and coyotes. I recall the onion, chili, lettuce, and cotton fields of La Mesilla

Valley. When I think of home, these creatures and food sources are a major part of my memories. When I visit, I know where to go if I want to explore the natural world of the borderlands. This inner pull is similar to my rattlesnake dreams, drawing me to walk along the river where I mark the changing course of the Rio Grande and learn where the bridges of home span the muddy stretches. This magnetism helps me to identify where the adobe ruins stand in La Mesilla Valley, thirty years after I first found the row of migrant worker huts as a boy.

I do not believe in the loss of home. An earthquake or other natural disaster can wipe out the town of our origins and it will still be there. Our private sounds and memories tell us where home lies eternally. Navajo people believe sacred ground must be earned. You are not born into a family and automatically given a place in the world. You must earn it. As you pay for it, the joys and sorrows that grow on sacred ground are identified for you as the citizens of your place on earth. You can celebrate or mourn the area where you grew up, with its stage of autobiographical failures and triumphs, but you have earned them and can't abandon them completely. The Navajos say it comes down to belief. The things you believe in are the factors that will protect or diminish your origins and your home.

October 14, 1934: The most damaging dust storm to hit El Paso shifted tons of sand from the barren desert onto city streets. The area was covered for several hours and everything came to a stop. Several cars were involved in accidents as the thick waves of sand kept drivers from seeing where they were going. Major streets downtown were closed due to drifts of sand, averaging two feet in thickness. Power lines came down and the Rio Grande turned a soft brown, its busy waters churning the mud on its way south. Huge piles of tumbleweeds appeared against buildings, and clusters of them were removed by city workers, private citizens, anyone who could grab a rake or shovel; some even used their bare hands and risked being cut by the dry weeds. Dust hung in the air for two days, immersing the city in a brown fog that made thousands sick, increased the crime rate for forty-eight hours (the dust a perfect shield for robbery and theft), and allowed an extra thousand or two illegal workers from Juárez to cross the river under its protection. Four people drowned in the Rio Grande, south of downtown, during those two days of dust, and eighteen murders were reported by the El Paso police. Ten of the victims were found covered in sand at various crime scenes around the city. Three building fires were reported, but two of them were extinguished by heavy rolls of dust that prevented the flames from breathing. The third fire resisted the brown particles and wiped out an old pickle factory in east El Paso.

I have been gone from the desert Southwest for twenty-five years, yet I continue to write about it. As the years go by, it is easier to acknowledge this landscape that "covers the past and hangs as the ember of thought/wisdom molded out of the falling world," as I wrote in one of my poems. I cannot let go of the Chihuahuan Desert, the Rio Grande, the Franklin and Organ Mountains, El Paso, and La Mesilla Valley—the falling world of my childhood and teenage years when I became a writer through the sheer immersion in an isolated yet vibrant place. I have lived elsewhere since 1979 and have written more poems about my home than I did when I lived in El Paso; biological time leads me to a new sense of home as a new century begins. The fact is, I have produced a large body of work that could not have been written if I had stayed in west Texas. This is hard to admit, but does not require sadness or romantic longings for home. It does call for occasional visits to see how Mexico, with its exciting culture and monumental problems, has transformed El Paso into an American version of itself. I had to leave my home two decades ago to be a writer who could face family issues, religious and spiritual conflicts, and the overwhelming presence of the desert from a safe distance—with a more objective view of how a childhood of isolation influenced the way I respond to the world and to re-create the border in my poems and stories. What this means is contained in what I have not created yet, though it can be found in what I have already written. It includes journeys home to witness the great transformations and conflicts taking place from San Diego, California, to Brownsville, Texas—political, economic, and environmental forces that point to the border where I grew up as a stage for the unfolding of the future of the United States and Mexico.

I walk along the Rio Grande at the millennium and it is not the same river, flowing steadily, then drying up before the next surge of water retraces its course. The Great River, to borrow Paul Horgan's phrase, is a line of water that traces and surrounds every conceivable problem and some of the solutions that New Mexico, Texas, and Mexico face—illegal immigration, water rights, radioactive waste, and the struggle to find new ways to attract outside investment and tourism to an area that traditionally has been one of the poorest in North America. The cottonwoods in La Mesilla Valley stand taller and thinner than when I last saw them as a young man. Much of the desert where I wandered as a boy is gone, replaced by strip malls and new housing that cover the trails I used to explore alone. In the middle of this growth, the tragedy of Mexico expands across the invisible border to reinforce a social and cultural poverty—a timeless erosion that eats away at the metropolitan region of El Paso and Juárez. Both legal and illegal workers from Mexico continue to cross, and I find more houses in El Paso with iron bars on the windows. Even the neighborhood where I grew up, with the exception of my mother's house, is saturated with the protective bars. Why has my mother not barred hers yet? Nostalgia for a time when there was less crime? More men, women, and children are coming across the border to take jobs U.S. citizens don't want. The average salary of working people in the area remains one of the lowest in the country. Poverty, crime, and the disappearing desert result in distrust and segregated neighborhoods. These stark but complex images are the first I see each time I visit.

A 1999 national survey found that Texas and New Mexico were the forty-eighth and forty-ninth worst places to live in this country. This conclusion was based on the quality of education, jobs, and the crime rate, but a May 2001 survey found El Paso to be the twelfth safest city in the United States—one of the best towns in one of the worst states, George W. Bush's legacy in Texas, long established before he became president. El Paso is the state's most isolated city, lying six hundred miles west of Austin and San Antonio, and to have it declared a safe place in a notoriously backward state says a great deal about the insulation the Chihuahuan Desert offers from the rest of the Lone Star state. These two surveys also represent the contradictions on the border: Low wages, a low cost of living, and an illegal, underground economy characterize a city that prefers to keep things that way, although one look across the international bridges on Stanton and Santa Fe streets reveals a different story, that of Mexico's rapid, unstoppable expansion north of the Rio Grande, and the source of a militarized border.

The June 11, 2001, issue of *Time* magazine features a major section on my home. "Welcome to Amexica" is the large headline, its letters painted in red, white, and blue, plus the red and green of Mexico. Two Mexican American children playing with colorful toys smile from the cover. I shake my head in the Minneapolis airport, where I first spot the new issue, because I've seen this media dance over the border many times before. The subtitle declares, "The border is vanishing before our eyes, creating a new world for all of us." Major news organizations like *Time,* ABC News, and several Internet media centers proclaim a week-long focus on illegal immigration, the drug wars, NAFTA, and the blending of everything American with everything Mexican. One *Time* reporter proclaims, "Salsa is more popular than ketchup; Salma Hayek is bigger than Madonna—and the border is everywhere!" The national media act as if life on the border is a brand-new phenomenon—or the latest Ricky Martin tune you can dance to.

To draw the reader into the long articles about life in Nogales, Laredo, Matamoros, and Juárez, *Time*'s editors highlight what they consider to be flabbergasting facts about the region in the post-NAFTA madness: The Wal-Mart in Laredo, population 193,000, is the highest grossing one per square foot in the United States; the border population is growing at almost twice the national rate; 31 percent of all tuberculosis cases are found in the four border states; apprehension of illegal aliens through March 2001 dropped 24 percent from the year before. Maps and charts of the New Frontier, or La Nueva Frontera, show key cities like San Diego and El Paso and are dotted with those well-known *Time* magazine polls on whether Canada is more important to the well-being of the United States than Mexico, which country has more of an impact on Americans, and, the one that stands out for me, "Do you think it should be easier or harder for people to cross the border into the United States?" Fifty-three percent of the people polled decided the already highly militarized and dangerous border should be made harder to cross from the Mexican side. Wal-Mart can make millions of dollars each month in Laredo and keeps its doors open to Mexican shoppers every night of the week, but the 53 percent who want to make it harder to come across illegally represent a growing attitude in a region torn by differences that a treaty like NAFTA will never change. Let's take those Mexican dollars but only if the cashiers can see some green cards? I don't know how many extra copies of the June 11 issue of *Time* sold as a result of ABC's nightly news stories on the border, but by June 18, Amexica is forgotten by the national media, as stories on President Bush's misbehaving daughters take the spotlight away from those late-night Wal-Mart shoppers in Nuevo Laredo.

My parents, sisters, and nephews live in the midst of great chaos and change. They don't have to read about it in the national media, as I often do. These days my family can't even use the border Spanish we were raised to speak. When my sisters, who are all teachers in the public schools, use words like *palomitas, carro, tenny shoes,* and other bilingual mutations, their fellow teachers scold them and try to correct their Spanish. These defenders of traditional Spanish, often young men and women born in Mexico but educated in the United States and now working here, refuse to acknowledge calo—the border speech Chicanos love and identify as a part of their culture—because this language represents the union of people who share their lives on the border.

A perfect example appeared when I overheard a Mexican American woman cashier in a busy cafeteria in El Paso tell her coworker to answer the phone by the cash register because she was too busy waiting on customers and the lights on the receiver "estan blinkiando." It was an old telephone with blinking lights for the different phone lines. I was paying for my food and saw the lights, then heard her say "estan blinkiando," so I knew I was home again. Blinkiando is the invisible border that crosses into the backyard of every member of my family, blinking from English to Spanish, then back again. It would have fit on the cover of *Time*—Amexica Blinkiando!—political and cultural conflicts perhaps too overwhelming for most writers of the desert to address in their poems, stories, and essays as they leave it to the national media to analyze why the border constantly flashes signals that it is okay to live in a prosperous region that really doesn't want its thriving citizens there.

After reading the border feature in *Time,* I grieve for what is gone, but this is nothing new for a writer. Growing older is the companion to the universal cycle of watching the past become dust, grasping this pollen by writing about a place where I no longer fit. Since 1979 I have written from Denver, San Antonio, Chicago, and now Minneapolis, needing these cities to be able to yearn for the desert from afar. When I admit "there is no limit to returning," I go back to search for what I have not seen before, what I overlooked in fleeing. I want solid trails cut through an arroyo I used to explore as a boy. I want to touch the cracked bark of the cottonwoods along the Rio Grande because "tomorrow I will see another kind of growth." What the invisible border gives, it takes away with the turbulent blending of the blinking populations of El Paso and Juárez, the brown and white faces becoming one profile. They now populate one city, one metropolitan region that is more Mexican than anything else. New elements of border life blend with the old and writers will be there to find them, despite the reality that the past century has changed their home forever.

One of the most common questions I am asked when I give talks on autobiographical writing is, "Where are you from?" When I answer "El Paso, Texas," I always get a handful of people raising their eyebrows as if to say, "Oh, that's out in the middle of nowhere," or "Oh, yeah, I drove through there once. Those brown mountains are amazing, but I didn't really like the place. There is nothing to do there." For most of my adult life, I agreed with these reactions; I wanted them to be the answers I gave from the city in which I resided in at the time. It has taken twenty-two years of living elsewhere, almost as many years as I lived in El Paso, to conclude that I grew up in an isolated place that had a great deal to offer me with its abundant human and animal life, a place where great, historic events of exploration and conquest took place, only to have them return as contrived notions from tourist bureaus searching for more dollars. Welcome to Amexica, land of rewritten history, where the Spaniard and the conquered Indian are noble and where the enormous illegal immigrant population is supposed to remain invisible. The bureaus don't want that working force to block entrances to popular museums, only to sweep their floors at midnight when all the tourists are gone.

My home contains an environmental, historical, and cultural richness I could not appreciate as a withdrawn boy who loved to collect fossils and dig under tumbleweeds during his lonely hikes through the desert. For two decades after I moved away, I told friends I left El Paso because there was nothing there for me. The more I believed this, the deeper I buried its cultural forces under the desert. It was easy to write about the landscape itself and how I explored it as a boy, but it was harder to write about my Catholic upbringing, the racism in the public schools, and how a Chicano should relate to Mexican nationals who, for the most part, saw my border upbringing and its contradictions of trying to be Mexican and a U.S. citizen at the same time as ridiculous. What the hell was I doing north of the international bridge when my family and I, and millions of other Chicanos who identified with sixties protest movements, were calling for a rebirth of our Aztec-Mexican roots?

Now I want to dig up the hidden landscapes of family and race, while I feel the tightening tensions of an invisible, international border that the U.S. media finds so captivating, as if spotlighting the border will help to find solutions to centuries-old problems. I had to go away and grow older to finally admit that my home has always been a life-giving, spiritually sustaining place. Too many people dismiss it as the land of the illiterate, the frontier of desperate people, or the breeding ground for the next generation of drug lords. They make these conclusions because they know nothing about the area. Or they play the tourist game of romanticizing life in the Southwest. This has resulted in the rise of heritage tourism, the ability of southwestern states to rewrite history for economic rewards. In cities like Albuquerque, El Paso, and Tucson, this means millions of tourist dollars are made by misinterpreting and romanticizing the exploration, conquest, and settling of the West—not the newest or most profound revelation when it comes to the story of this country, but in the Southwest, heritage tourism takes on new meaning when museums are built to glorify nuclear war, to salute the art of capturing illegal immigrants, and to show how American might defeated "deranged" revolutionary heroes who never needed U.S. help to stage their own downfalls in the first place. The results are strange tourist centers that draw outsiders to give them a distorted view of southwestern life as they leave their dollars in museum gift shops and go home weighed down with pounds of Indian jewelry around their necks.

I studied heritage tourism on the border during several trips I took to the Southwest in 1999 through 2001. What I found in museums and art galleries differs greatly from what *Time* magazine featured. After returning to my home as a native, and playing tourist from the point of view of someone who grew up in the desert of Juan de Oñate, Robert Oppenheimer, and Pancho Villa, I conclude that beautiful Indian ruins, the horrors of Trinity and Los Alamos, and racist stereotypes from south of the border could take place only along the timeless current of the Rio Grande because New Mexico and west Texas have magnetized their bloody past and present with the forces of once powerful civilizations, weapons of mass destruction, and revolutionary movements that tore international boundaries open. These tumultuous events have been calling to people to gather and cross at the border—dead Spanish conquistadores lying alongside vanished tribes and the buried secrets of government knowledge.

Many people I meet in El Paso today didn't grow up there, though they control Chamber of Commerce and Tourist Bureau offices. Their generalizations about Mexican food, the "beauty" of the desert, and their ways of shrugging off racial and class separations were shaped by their lives elsewhere and their acceptance of heritage tourism as an attractive, monetary truth to add to border liquor, Mexican food, stripper bars, and beautiful vistas with a turquoise coyote howling at the moon on t-shirts, cups, necklaces, and expensive pendants.

Each time I go home, the boy who isolated himself by wandering the desert reemerges to give me something new. The more I visit, the more that mute boy shifts from mourning what can never be relived to one who celebrates the place that made him who he is, despite the dynamics of an external manipulation and its realignment of life in El Paso and other southwestern cities. Tucking away parts of my past helped me find the courage to leave the area, though it took years to get rid of the anger over a life I didn't understand there. Now I wander a place undergoing enormous changes, while parts of it hang onto a decaying environment influenced by poverty, illegal immigration, and dying cultural traditions. Amid these shattering dramas, I return with love and compassion as I try to understand what has happened to my beloved Chihuahuan Desert and Rio Grande.

December 14, 1947: The hardest dust storm to hit El Paso in several years uncovered fourteen headstones at Concordia cemetery. As the oldest graveyard in El Paso, in constant use since 1851, Concordia has layer upon layer of ancient graves, tombs, and headstones. Besides sweeping tons of sand across the old grave markers, the storm lifted tons more to reveal the previously unknown markers near the southeast corner of the huge cemetery. Most of the markings on the headstones eroded long ago, but three sites were identified as belonging to Rosario Vargas, 1872–1890; Pedro Ochoa, 1879–1890; and Maria Lopez, 1872–1890. City and cemetery records were found for Ochoa and Lopez, the documents stating the two deceased were drowning victims of a previously unknown Rio Grande flood of 1890. No details could be found on Vargas or the eleven other unidentified graves.

During my first trip to El Paso after the turn of the century, its familiar and strange characteristics bring back memories of becoming a writer. This recollection comes from the routine I had as a boy during hot summers. One July night as I lay in my bedroom, I went through my nightly habit of opening the window to let the cool desert breeze blow in through the screen. I turned on the tiny radio I kept on the nightstand near the bed, its volume low as Wolfman Jack played the latest Top 40 hits. I lay in the dark and stared at the blackness of the room, waiting for the distant sound of trains. The railroad tracks were three miles south of the neighborhood, and the whistle and faraway rumble of the engines came around midnight. By then, my parents and sisters were asleep in other parts of the house. It was soothing to lie in the quiet room and wait for the familiar sounds. I wondered where the trains went, wanting to know where the tracks ended—what state, what city? As any eleven-year-old might fantasize, I wondered how old I would be before I could jump onto one of those trains and be taken to a new place. I had fun during the summers away from school, but the feeling of wanting to go somewhere else intensified when I listened to the trains.

This night took a different turn. As soon as the distant whistle died away and the tracks stopped their metallic rhythm, I heard the cry of a coyote. Startled, I sat up, turned off the radio, and listened. The second wail came through the window and sounded like the animal was in the front yard. I was scared because I had never heard a coyote so close to the house, and it was rare to hear coyotes in the desert surrounding the neighborhood. I went to the window and peered across the street. No homes had been built there, our house being the edge of a new housing development. Fifty yards from our front door, the empty lots turned into the desert hills I explored alone during the hot days.

When my eyes adjusted to the dark, I thought I saw something moving at the top of the hill. It was a clear night with stars glittering across the desert sky. The coyote howled again and sent shivers down my back. I did not go outside to get a better look, even though my room had a door to the front porch. Two more cries were followed by a stark silence, and I went back to bed. The following day, I wrote what I clearly remember to be my first poem. I wrote about the railroad and the coyote—the train pulling me away from El Paso and the chilling cries of the coyote keeping me in the desert.

Tortas Locas

In his essay "The Place, the Region, and the Commons," poet Gary Snyder tells us, "The childhood landscape is learned on foot, and a map is inscribed in the mind—trails and pathways . . . going out farther and wider." He writes about the perception of young children and how we carry a picture of the terrain within us, things we learn between the ages of six and nine. Snyder concludes, "Revisualizing that place with its smells and textures, walking through it again in your imagination, has a grounding and settling effect." I may have internalized the terrain of the desert at a very young age, but it was the unlocking of my creativity at age eleven that got the tides turning.

Trying to find traces of these maps, I visit the recently opened El Paso History Museum, a small building on the east side of town that used to be a steakhouse. Old habits are hard to break; I think, "Only in El Paso would a restaurant building become a history museum and still look like a restaurant from the outside." An exhibit of photographs reveals what the town looked like before my family came to El Paso. I stare at panoramic images stretched across the museum walls, and a line from one of my poems emerges—"The heart is a self-portrait." It is also a downtown street in a yellow photograph from 1916, buildings I never saw before they were turned over to the ghosts. I squint as I study the tiny carriages and Model Ts an old camera managed to capture. That tower over in the corner. Four children trapped there by a woman who lit a torch in 1914. The heart is not a historian, simply an oxygen machine in the old hospital where I was born, the building rising tall in the other photograph. The first movement of my legs was the same as the other babies born that September day in 1952. The hospital is now gone, thirty-two drawers of unexplained cadavers bulldozed, without a report filed. The heart is a petrified tree hiding under the bricks of the growing town, branches that held sparrows and pigeons under an evening sun, where the man dressed in black first appeared, 1904. Blink closer. Right there in the huge, yellow photograph, he leans against the last cottonwood before it was removed, the public hangings banned from the streets, executions of Mexicans and Tewa Indians moved to the basement of the building cropped out of the photo.

The heart is the survivor of rewritten history. It is the yellowing image of return, another photograph showing a man wading in the shallow fountain in San Jacinto Plaza, wrestling or feeding the alligators kept there in the fifties and early sixties. The fountain in the plaza cascaded dirty water, rose above the crowd watching five alligators trapped there. They moved heavily toward the trash and food thrown at them, one or two crunching coke cans, no one from the city keeping the tormentors away. One year, they found one dead alligator with three arrows in its neck, finally sent the rest to the zoo. Downtown El Paso lost its monsters, replaced by hookers hanging around the bus stops when I walked by as a boy, searching for something to replace the alligators, waiting for the plaza to become a miniature Christmas village. The tall tree ignited in white and blue lights the night my parents took me to see Santa. I realized there was no such thing as St. Nick when the guy in the suit said something ugly to the little girl ahead of me, his impatience disappearing as I stared, thousands of lights and Christmas villages blinking into a city, the fountain frozen as the look on that Santa who noticed I knew what he was. I skipped my turn on his lap to find the alligators in the pool waiting for me to hang over the railing so they could respond to my movement, slap the water with their long, heavy tails so lights couldn't settle onto their moving mouths.

This exhibit also hides a clock behind a brick wall, its secret mechanism ticking since 1932. It has been hiding in the bank building erected over the old courthouse that replaced the saloon built over the adobe wall that survived the destruction of the first pueblo. I want to repeat that last sentence to myself because it is the oral pronouncement of border history, one culture on top of another, crushing and reforming itself to make a whole new civilization come alive on the banks of the Rio Grande. The layer upon layer makes me leave the museum. Before I go, I stare at another nine-foot-wide panoramic photo of downtown, 1918. The mud pueblo is somewhere underneath. I try to pinpoint it—right there, in the old photo pulled out of the archives where the heart does not belong. These close-ups of old El Paso send me away from the city and on a quick drive to the Upper Valley where the river erases the controlling smell of enormous, ancient photographs.

It was reported in a November 4, 1994, article in the *El Paso Times* that researchers have found that tequila reduces radioactivity in living things. Several scientists in Russia imported several gallons of José Cuervo tequila from Mexico and gave it to some survivors of the Chernobyl nuclear accident. These victims had lived hundreds of miles away but were suffering from radioactive poisoning over the years. A few gave birth to deformed children. The scientists reported that in some victims who drank several glasses of tequila, the effects of radioactive sickness diminished, though these patients remained ill over a period of time. They were weak, but their bodies showed signs of recovery, and some of the radioactive burns on their arms and legs disappeared. Further study was being conducted as the scientists awaited more deliveries of the fine Mexican drink.

I have driven along the Rio Grande hundreds of times, the river looking the same and often very different. It flows past a childhood of the desert and runs through my adult life elsewhere. As I cross the tall, yellow fields and head toward the irrigation canals of La Mesa, I am only four years old and turning fifty this year. I count the years: 1999, 2000, and 2001. The Rio Grande flies by, its dark waters high and fast as they force their power under concrete bridges used by populations that come and go. When the Border Patrol pulled the illegal immigrant out of the river, his face was gone, having returned to San Luis Matalon, where the hands of the one he loved waited for him. What is it that won't wait for the Rio Grande's drowning victim number seventeen for the month of July? How do we forgive the cracking mud between our fingers? The drowned man will never know how he made it home in time to become a terrible god arriving in the first flames of dawn, the dripping angels of blood and immigration spreading holy water over the town where Juan Melendez was born, then returned. The drowned man has seen it too often—the way the darkness interrupted his escape, the fleeing bats brushing his head as he drove into tomorrow, promising his family he would send money from the north. What fell asleep on the broken current and churned the crossing heart into sinking kingdoms of hope? How often did it hurt to open his hands and try to grab the barbed wire fence?

When a half dozen illegal aliens robbed a train west of El Paso in 1999, the railroad crew let them take what they wanted. The boxcars were broken open to reveal there was no food, only the heat of summer and seventy-nine dead bodies searching for water, riding the tracks as if the train whistle signaled it was finally a new country. The Rio Grande kept its course toward the southern mouth of freedom, and there were fourteen more drownings in the three weeks following the train assault.

What is beautiful but can't approach the water? How do we get it to come closer so we can all jump in and be swept to safety, our memories mushrooms to another life, the streets melting into the waterfall where every tribe that jumped in survived, until they staggered into the horizon with glowing bodies that could never be healed from too much water that sent them to a world of peace? What is this knowledge in the beating, swollen chest? How do we move to say we forgot it long ago? Who invented drowning and promised the water would always flow?

I drive for more than an hour, walk for one more, and don't want anything to come near me. I hike through the ocotillo field near Fort Selden State Park, then stumble upon the bricked wall of the public restroom and run inside. After I am done, I exit and look up. High in the darkness where the wall meets the roof, a cluster of gray bats sleeps and wakes, sleeps and wakes, their neatly folded wings resembling the pages I threw away when I tried to write the truth. What if I never go back to El Paso? Will the double agent of summer twist in the dry wind and reveal where the massacre of the pueblo people took place? I don't want anything to get in the way of finding what I have missed. A roadrunner has followed me into the park, its sharp head watching for anything that moves, the huge rattler that crossed the road not coiling in time as the bird strikes. Two of the bats open their eyes at me, their rat features in trance showing me how the man in danger comes out of the desert, slices open the barrel cactus, and takes a drink.

I pass the sharp ocotillo and salt cedars near Chamberino, New Mexico, and stop between two cottonwoods near the great bend, north of Hatch. It is the same, but the river and its trees have been transformed. As I drive across one of the concrete bridges near Canutillo, the broken adobe walls of two houses and the dancing graffiti on their mud slabs greet me. I am back and I am gone. I spot several boys splashing in the low water and can't tell if they are crossing, fleeing, or simply playing. There is no rain of white cotton from the trees that will outlast their friendship and outlive the torn buildings. I keep driving and cross, and they keep coming on.

The white rain from the cottonwoods kisses the salt of their skin, then floats toward the highway, their rivers meandering toward the other side where no one has set foot in years. The white cotton from the trees hovers across the arroyo that bends north, away from the Rio Grande, and keeps footprints on this side of the razor wire, away from the agricultural valley. Decades ago, someone bit into a whole head of lettuce from these fields and dropped the wet leaves here, the hard design of bitterness planting itself for the future harvest. The white rain from the cottonwoods keeps falling over the five abandoned buildings in the tiny town, whose name I do not know, the only street illustrated by black graffiti on the crumbling walls, one building proclaiming "Beware of Rattlesnakes." The white mist hits the ground when the locked door is kicked in and another rain becomes a forgotten road where adrenaline is an unlaced boot dragged out of the ruins by a silent tarantula.

I find the arranged stones in the middle of the clearing at the edge of town. They look like they were placed there by someone wanting to release something I should have freed years ago, but this person fled before anything emerged from the pattern. The smooth stones are covered in bright green moss, others marked in white chalk lines moving toward the center to tell me to pay attention. The stones were set this way to open the ground, not cover it, at least two dozen tossed yards away; the digger ran out of time as some of the stones rolled to replace what had been dug up. Then I saw the pattern emerge from what was left—eleven stones in the shape of a hungry dog, two the eyes of the carpenter who took the decaying lumber away, six others the rocks from a fallen sky that were shattered here to announce the church was built in the wrong place. It should have risen on the other side of the cotton field where the one stone of blue moss grows by itself, its round-ness the top of the head of someone needing help standing up. My attempt at interpreting the stones that emerge from the desert soil forces me back to the city and an area whose stones are the barrio walls of family destruc-tion and abandonment—histories surrounded by ruins and cemeteries where nothing rises, only disintegrates into hard ground where the remains of neighborhoods are as important as the desert.

The border guilt has to do with enjoying a wonderful breakfast in a Taco Cabana, one of my favorite fast-food Mexican restaurants in El Paso. I order huevos rancheros, the steaming rice and beans a great addition to the two over-easy eggs covered with hot sauce. I sip my coffee and enjoy the first good Mexican breakfast I have had in months, life in the northern arctic of Minnesota making it hard to find this kind of Mexican food. I take several bites and spot the boy. He is sitting at an empty table across from me, his mouth watering, his brown knees showing through his torn jeans. The Mexi-can boy has a starved look on his face and has been begging the few customers in the place for handouts. I have been too busy eating to notice him until he sits wearily, his mouth watering, his desperate eyes staring at my food. I stop in mid-bite and don't know what to do. I push my tray away and start to stand and reach for my wallet to give him some money, my guilt over savoring my food replacing the fine taste in my mouth. When I push my plate back, the boy jumps up quickly and runs out the door of the café, an employee shooing him out, my wallet frozen in my hands, the huevos rancheros sitting cold on the table.

In the summer months of 1939, El Sagrado Corazon Catholic Church in El Paso gave first confessions and holy communions to 3,812 Mexican boys and girls.

Of that number, 1,456 are known to be alive, all of them in their early seventies. Of this smaller number, 1,014 still live in El Paso and 442 are scattered over the United States and Mexico. Of the other 2,356 people, death certificates show 1,759 are buried in El Paso cemeteries and 92 are buried elsewhere. The remaining 505 boys and girls who were cleansed of their sins throughout the summer of 1939 are unaccounted for. Their names remain on the archival rolls of El Sagrado Corazon.

That same summer of 1939, the *El Paso Herald Post* ran four different short articles on UFO sightings in the deserts around the small city. The first documents strange lights witnessed by several people way out on old Paisano Drive near the river. The second story, appearing two days later, talks about oval-shaped vehicles spotted in the skies over the eastern slopes of the Franklin Mountains. The third interviews a Johnny Cervantes, who says he saw several flashes of light near San Lorenzo, in the lower valley, and swears his car radio went crazy with interference the night he sat in it and looked up at the lights. The fourth said the reporter could not get anyone from Fort Bliss to talk about the various sightings and listed a phone number of a local group of citizens who had been recording such sightings until one of their meetings was raided by military police, their scrapbooks confiscated, and the group shut down. Weeks of detailed examination of El Paso newspapers for 1938, the rest of 1939, and 1940 show not one single article about UFOs.

In the summer of 1892, seven mountain lions were shot in the Franklin Mountains after a rise in attacks on people. As the town of El Paso grew around the mountain, more of the wild animals came into contact with the growing population. In July of that year, six citizens of the town were attacked, one mauled to death. The dead lions were displayed in San Jacinto Plaza, their thin hides and huge heads hanging from two trees for everyone to examine.

The old building in one barrio is closed and boarded up, indecipherable graffiti on its broken walls lighting the quiet south El Paso neighborhood. The rusting sign above the chained door says Tortilla Productions. Nothing else. No clue as to what they produce. Plays? Performance poetry? Comedy? The structure is large enough to house a small theater, but it is not the kind of area most theatergoers would come to at night. The boundaries for that kind of art are finely drawn in the border town. I cross the dirt lot bristling with broken beer bottles, pieces of old glass crunching under my shoes, ringing like tiny bells that want to lift their familiar sound from the desolation of the area. Next door to Tortilla Productions is another closed business, El Alacrán Lounge. Alacrán—Spanish for scorpion. The Scorpion Lounge—a smaller concrete box not only barricaded, but reinforced. The double front doors and the one lone window on its side are covered with iron bars. The graffiti on this ruin can be easily read—Tu Madre Es Una Puta! Then, an odd grinning face next to the pronouncement. Blue paint—the most popular color for tagging around here. El Alacrán Lounge. The sting. The bite. The night of the lone woman sitting at the bar. El Alacrán. The dark figure of a man waiting in the parking lot.

I cross the street to get away from the lingering odor of beer and piss, the fine layer of broken beer glass singing under my feet again, the rhythm broken by the sudden flight of two pigeons I startle at curbside. Their gray bodies flush into the early sunlight and disappear over the roof of the third decaying spot, Tortas Locas. It used to be one of my favorite neighborhood cafes. Tortas Locas. The funny name for delicious Mexican food that stung my mouth and filled me with tastes I have missed. Closed. Locas no more. The rectangular glass window surprises me by surviving the abandonment. Long strips of heavy tape crisscross the window and make it hard to look inside. I peer through the glass, but the light won't illuminate the shattered counter and the two remaining stools, the others marking their disappearance by the holes in the concrete floor.

Suddenly, I hear the jingling horn of the Border Jumper, the new trolley that takes tourists across the border to Juárez. It is a compact motorized bus outfitted to look like one of the original trolleys that used to run on tracks connecting both countries before they became one. The Border Jumper passes two streets down from these ruins. It is a quick trip from the Convention Center to El Mercado in downtown Juárez. No one in El Paso has thought of creating a tour of devastated neighborhoods yet. It would be of interest to the wave of tourists that come here. After all, as I get into my car and move only two blocks east, I find La Paloma Café open—one of the best and oldest Mexican restaurants in El Paso, doing business before I was born, the old neon sign of a dove still hanging above the door. The tourists would love it, but to get to La Paloma would mean passing by Tortilla Productions, El Alacrán Lounge, and Tortas Locas.

They would not recognize the names of home the way I do when I leave south El Paso and drive toward Ysleta. Block after block of decaying businesses, most of them open and busy, crowd Paisano and Alameda streets. Sign after sign of colorful lettering and advertising make me forget the Border Jumper. I pass the Viva Villa Bar, Dulcería El Loco, Azteca Motors, the Chicken Coop Lounge, Chilo's Radiator, Barrio Motors, El Yaqui Auto Repair, and Mina's Old Fashioned Hog Cracklings, then slow down in front of a laundry and cleaners whose sign says "Zoot Suits Available Here." I know these places. Their language has been with me since my first poem about the train and coyote. Llanteria California, Cuba Glass and Windows, La Salsa Income Tax Service, Arriba Bail Bonds, the Pink Flamingo Motel, Lobo Communications, and Taqueria La Pila.

In an essay on creation myths, Native American poet Linda Hogan says we are drawn back to our origins by the pull of cells in our bodies. No matter where we are standing on the earth, these internal magnets of biological connection implant the belief there is always a home and we must go there. In the El Paso area, neon and hand-painted signs are crucial in connecting this human yearning to the current state of our origins. Mr. Poncho's Hamburgers, La Milpa Tortilla Factory, La Malinche Mexican Food, Baldo's Haircuts, Castro's Fix Flats, Autos Mas, Yonke Auto Salvage. Signs of survival and creation myths with their visual effect—a key element in El Paso has always been the power of what is visually revealed in the surreal heat. These images call us to return in the same manner birds migrate and return each winter and sea turtles swim to the same islands to lay their eggs, generation after generation. A nest of advertising signs is a weird reason for migration; it sounds crazy. Yet this time when I read the signs and think, "Only in El Paso," I welcome the words on the billboards. Acapulco Bakery, El Escandalo Dance Hall, Salud y Vida Weight Control. I quit looking when I spot Home Sweet Home Bank Repos. Hogan concludes, "We remember our ancestors and their lives in our cells. It is a deep and unspoken remembering." These memories are pulled out of the desert ground, their hidden profiles labeled with the alphabet of survival, poverty, and continuation—a lettering taken from English and Spanish to illustrate what has become of the town where I grew up, a musical alphabet that says more than a *Time* magazine cover ever will.

If writing about this place for decades means I am constantly re-creating my home, I can leave and go north again, not be around when the last boarded-up building is torn down or too many of those wild billboards are erased. If years of failed and triumphant poetry blend together to map a new course for the river and the streets of El Paso, I have said what I wanted in my work, the hidden landscapes of yesterday finally emerging into the desert air. It is a gift and a loss. It is "history being overlooked" so I can live along the muddy ribbons of water and be able to say I wrote too soon, composed too late, and the twentieth century has ended. Yet my work was written at the exact instant the Rio Grande shifted course, the years it took for house after house and business after business to go up or down. I saw the river nourish its proud line of cottonwoods. I stood by the Great River and knew. Only then did I allow the trees to bend close to the water.

Rest Stop

I pull into the Sierra Ladrona rest stop fifty miles south of Albuquerque and my car radio says one hundred and two degrees will be the high today. The two o'clock sun feels hotter when I park next to a station wagon with Colorado plates, its passengers strolling up the wood platform to the bathrooms. I like the Sierra Ladrona stop and have used its clean facilities before, the structure built out of enormous wood beams that make the shelter resemble a long ship, perhaps Noah's ark floating across miles of barren desert. From the parking lot, the entire structure rises at an angle to more than ten feet off the desert ground, its wooden floor supported by massive stilts. It is one of the few rest stops of this design I have found on the highways of the Southwest.

I step out into the waves of heat that want to push my body back into the air-conditioned car. The sign on the platform says "Beware of Rattlesnakes." In the middle of a hot day, they are not a problem, but perhaps night travelers feel safer knowing the bathrooms they are about to enter are suspended high above the nocturnal wanderings of diamondbacks. When I drive through the state, I always make it a point to observe these places, which often reveal the temperament of fellow travelers and conditions of the roads, and give me the sense I am almost at my destination. Rest stops measure my progress across the desert.

I take a piss in the spotless men's room; the tiled floor has been recently mopped and the trash bins cleared of overflowing paper towels. A father helps his small son into one of the stalls, and an elderly man in a Dodgers baseball cap washes his hands over the shiny sink. When I'm done, I wash mine as the elderly man pulls at least six towels from the dispenser. The huge, crumpled ball he throws into the basket slowly expands inside it as he moves out the door.

I have been driving for several hours and don't want to get into the car yet, so I step off the wooden platform to read the historical marker nearby. Whoever cleans the bathrooms must not be responsible for state markers, because three McDonald's hamburger wrappers stick out of the sand and lean against the base of the old sign. As I get closer to read the faded yellow words, a large collar lizard darts from behind the marker, crosses the sand and mesquite, then stops by the wire fence separating the road from hundreds of square miles of pure desert. Lizards were as abundant as flies when I was growing up in west Texas, but this is the first I have seen in many years.

The marker says I am standing on the north end of La Jornada del Muerto, the waterless stretch of desert notorious for being the graveyard of Spanish conquistadores and other explorers coming north from Mexico. This part of La Jornada is singled out as El Pasaje de Fray Cristóbal, the route of a sixteenth-century Spanish priest who converted thousands of Pueblo Indians and was then turned upon in the bloody Pueblo Revolt of 1589. Cristóbal's head was cut off by the people and, as a warning, displayed on a pole in one of the pueblos that was generous to the Spaniards. Of course the marker doesn't mention the revolt or reveal the priest's fate, but instead focuses on how the blending of Spanish and native cultures made New Mexico what it is today. I stumbled upon the facts of Cristóbal's death in a history book years ago, facts most historical markers would never include, because true stories about this area can undo the romantic atmosphere promoted by tourist bureaus to attract the owners of motor homes and RVs. This sign says the area is named for the Sierra Ladrona Mountains twenty miles behind me, one peak the favorite hiding place for bandits in the Wild West of the mid-nineteenth century. The sign claims the Sierra Ladronas contain a lost cache of gold outlaws hid there one hundred and fifty years ago.

The heat sends me back to the car, and the big lizard shoots under the fence and disappears. As I let the engine idle before getting back on I-25 toward Albuquerque, the "Beware of Rattlesnakes" sign shakes gently in the scorching breeze. Reading it again reminds me of a snake story that writer Barry Lopez told a group of us a few months ago. He said the most horrifying rattlesnake encounter he'd heard of involved a young woman camping with friends in Arizona. One night, after several beers, she had to pee and stepped twenty yards from the campfire. She pulled her jeans down, did her business, and then felt the painful jolt of a rattlesnake as it bit her ankle from behind, her pants still down. In the darkness, she never saw it and came up screaming. Her friends ran to her and dragged her into the light of the fire to discover that a six-foot diamondback rattler still had its fangs stuck in her leg. As she screamed and struggled with the thick, wriggling creature that wouldn't let go, two of the men killed it with rocks. They rushed her to a hospital, and the doctor had to cut the huge head of the dead rattler from her leg. She recovered after several weeks in intensive care.

This incident is in contrast with an experience I had two years ago on one of my winter travels through New Mexico. In weather opposite of the present summer heat, I pulled into a rest stop ten miles south of Santa Fe. This station is designated the New Mexico Information Center because the visitor's headquarters is a room full of thousands of free brochures, catalogs, and documents on the wonders of the state. Volunteers stand behind a counter and point out the latest Taos gallery publication or a pamphlet on the most obscure archaeological site in Tortugas. Everything is free, and I have stopped there many times to gather armloads of informative publications on New Mexico. I dump the brochures and maps in the car and sort them later.

On this occasion, I pull in to go to the bathroom and check out the latest freebies. When I park, I notice the sign that says "Bathrooms Out of Order" and the row of four portable toilets, their bright turquoise cylinders rising against the bright snow. I can't believe it. New Mexico is known for some of the best, cleanest, and most efficient rest stops in the western United States. I hate portable potties, but I need to go after several hours of driving. I pass several "Watch For Ice" signs and shiver inside the awful, stinking chamber. No one has cleaned out the one I choose, and it is backed up.

I do my business and slide across the ice to get to the visitor's center. An elderly couple stands nervously behind the counter. I can't inspect the hundreds of brochures on the wall racks because a tourist is holding the state volunteers hostage with a barrage of questions and comments.

"Are there snakes in New Mexico?" the middle-aged woman asks in a shrill voice. "We don't have snakes in Minnesota."

Minnesota! I blink at the wall of publications. I live in Minnesota and here is a fellow citizen following me all the way to the desert.

The man behind the counter starts to answer her question but is interrupted.

"What kind of art do the Indians sell in Taos? Is it local Indian art or national Indian art? We have lots of art in Minnesota, but I don't know where our Indians come from."

I place my hand on the nearest attractive pamphlet. The volunteers try to explain the culture in Taos, but again, "Where is Route 66? Why is it so famous? I came on Interstate 40. Is that Route 66 today?"

The elderly man gets in a few words about Route 66 and we hear barking dogs outside.

The woman from Minnesota turns to the door. "Oh, those are my four dogs in the van. I take them everywhere I go. They're in a special carrier. A few years ago, I was rear-ended and dogs went flying everywhere."

Silence at the counter as she picks up a handful of catalogs and walks to the door. I have moved to the other side of the small room by now.

"By the way," she pauses. "I noticed the casinos down the highway. Do the Indians here own the casinos? In Minnesota, all the Indians own the casinos."

She doesn't wait for an answer and opens the door to muffled barking in the parking lot. When I turn to make sure she is gone, I notice the sign by the water fountain on the wall: Do Not Drink the Water. I grab a couple dozen brochures I've never seen before and am back on the icy highway within minutes.

The memory of that winter encounter with the curious woman from Minnesota fades as I recall the most recent developments on the rest-stop front. I recently read a news story about Starbucks planning to open counters in hundreds of rest stops across the United States. So much for quiet, isolated breaks from long-distance driving. Will they serve hot coffee in this terrible heat? How will they choose rest stops at which to do business? I also read that several computer companies plan to open "web stops" at rest areas. When they are installed, you will be able to pull over and log on at computer kiosks located at stops throughout the country. You can check your e-mail or even book a hotel from out in the middle of nowhere. The terminals will be right there, in the one-hundred-and-four-degree temperatures, the radio now says. Stretch your legs, go to the bathroom, then surf the Net. I picture a Starbucks and rows of computer screens here as the boy and father I saw in the restroom run down the platform to their car, several yellow jackets buzzing around their heads. The boy shouts something I can't make out through my closed window, and the father yanks the cap off his head, trying desperately to swat away three or four huge wasps that descend on him. The mother waiting inside the car waves her arms and grabs the upset boy. The father slams his door and wasps circle the car. Two or three of them have the audacity to stray across my windshield, reminding me that I saw several yellow jackets hovering under the wooden beams near the bathrooms.

I get on the highway north and leave the Sierra Ladrona rest stop behind. After several days in Albuquerque, I will head back to El Paso and pull into the southbound Sierra Ladrona rest stop on the other side of the highway, where a "Beware of Rattlesnakes" sign greets me, the identical wooden structure cleared of yellow jackets, but inhabited by two tiny lizards who flash across the parking lot as I climb the platform toward the air-conditioned, working restrooms.

Millennium Tour

I wander through El Paso near the end of the century, amazed at how it has become part of Mexico. Downtown is no longer downtown El Paso. It is an extension of Juárez. The tienditas, used clothing stores, and Mexicans selling their goods on the sidewalk are straight out of a busy Juárez scene. The crowds are one hundred percent Mexican, shoppers from across the border who cross legally to buy American goods every day of the week. Of course, illegals dodge from store to store looking for work and watching for green La Migra vans, hiding if one passes down the street. Anglos from El Paso don't shop here. I strain to spot a single one. Mass killings in Juárez make international news.

Instead of finding the forty or fifty bodies drug informers claim are buried on a ranch south of Juárez, the FBI and Mexican police find four bodies. Two of them are identified as a lawyer and his client, a member of a Juárez drug cartel who testified in an El Paso court a few days before they both disappeared. Has this incident scared Anglos away from downtown?

It is 1999, and Peter, my best friend from my El Paso days who now lives in Washington, D.C., e-mails that his mother has passed away. I have known her and her son since I was five years old, longer than anyone else outside my immediate family. I have been trying to contact my father for a year; his habit of moving around town without leaving a forwarding address is effective in keeping his children at a distance. My parents' divorce is going on eighteen years as everybody braces themselves for the millennium. I try old phone numbers but can't find my father. Generations are passing as Y2K turns out to be a bust.

I live in Minneapolis and teach at the University of Minnesota, whose football team made me laugh by being invited to the Sun Bowl in the first year of my teaching. The team had its first winning season in decades and waited to be invited to a more prestigious bowl for postseason play. When everyone passes them by and El Paso extends an invitation, several racist news stories appear in Twin Cities papers. I hear the comments about Mexicans on campus and read columns by local sports writers who accompany the team to El Paso in late December. They are stunned at the thousands of shacks across the river in Juárez, the colonias of poverty visible to the team every day from the Sun Bowl practice fields at UTEP, my alma mater. Minnesotans have never seen such a sight. One reporter describes the Gopher's strict routine of practicing, then making the frantic hop to the hotel on secure buses, afraid packs of illegal aliens might jump them. I thought these guys were supposed to be tough football players, though they admit enjoying the visit to the Tony Lama boot factory in El Paso, a traditional rite for every school that plays in the Sun Bowl. I stare at the photo in the *Minneapolis Star Tribune* showing a bunch of grimacing football players wearing cowboy boots that don't fit.

One sports writer focuses on the rabid Gopher fans and families who paid thousands of dollars for special tourist packages to El Paso. He says many are afraid to venture into the wilds of the border. He interviews those who feel ripped off because there is no place to have fun in El Paso. "There's nothing but desert around here," one fan says. "How can they stand it?" Another asks, "Where does everybody go? Downtown El Paso is dead!" She has her answer when she follows hundreds of Minnesotans, who take their chances by crossing into Juárez to get drunk and buy cheap leather goods. I wonder how many homes in Minneapolis and St. Paul will display Elvis Presley on black velvet paintings in the coming year. The reporter goes on and on about the poverty everywhere you look and concludes that Minnesotans who did not spend their hard-earned money to come to El Paso were better off staying home and watching the game on television. This attitude continues as racist article after racist article appears over the next two weeks. No one in the Twin Cities raises an alarm at the tone the sports writers take toward this bowl appearance "on the Mexican border," where proud Gopher fans have never dared set foot before. Minnesotan readers of these articles and viewers of sports broadcasts must believe whatever they are told about the border. Reality shaves Gopher arrogance down to size when the team and the few thousand Gopher fans who attend are wiped out by the University of Oregon by a score of thirty-four to twelve. What a way to end their great year—stuck in El Paso for a few days of dangerous desert, menacing illegal aliens, and Mexican food that has many of them spending hotel time in the bathroom. I flew incognito into El Paso during this whole mess; there were no football fans on my flight, no one suspecting I teach at the proud university that got a taste of border culture.

To forget Minnesotans on the border, I drive north into La Mesilla Valley. Instead of following my usual route through agricultural back roads, I take Doniphan Drive toward Las Cruces. As I pass through Anthony, New Mexico, a large crowd of Mexicans on a street corner draws my attention. About fifty of them are waiting for the doors of the Nueva Jerusalem Temple to open. Several Stars of David are painted on the clean, well-groomed building—a Jewish temple for Mexicans. I can tell most of the crowd is from Mexico by the way the men, caballeros, are dressed. Their starched white shirts and cowboy hats are not the fashion of Chicanos from the United States. I slow down as more of them cross the busy highway toward Nueva Jerusalem, with its Jewish symbols and weekend services in Spanish.

The enthusiasm of these Jewish Mexicans and a piece of news I hear convince me that El Paso has been living in the next century for a long time. The historical, centuries-old "clash of cultures" is now a "mutation" of cultures, where the fine lines between old Mexico, New Mexico, and Mexican American life have been erased forever. The big announcement is that the Texas Parks and Wildlife Department has granted the city $750,000 to develop the first phase of a regional river park. A river walk on the Rio Grande! Officials want to model it after the famous River Walk in San Antonio. That attractive tourist magnet is located downtown and flows through a busy shopping mall and finely landscaped canals. El Pasoans want one of their own. The development grant calls for a nine-mile trail system along the Rio Grande that would begin at an already established park in the Upper Valley, not far from the Jewish Mexican temple, and extend to Vinton farther north. What about the fact that the nine-mile stretch is one of the busiest crossing areas for illegal aliens and drug smugglers and runs through some of the most desolate places in the Upper Valley? Editorials in the local paper claim it will "surely attract many hikers, cyclists, and pleasure walkers." Pleasure walkers? There is no such thing as a pleasure walk on the border. It is too hostile and ineffectively fenced off. The wild landscape along the river is an obstacle for any hiker.

The river walk idea has taken the last shreds of nostalgia for my home-town and paved over them with development money. There is a great deal of snickering from area residents who know the river walk proposal will never work, because assaults will be frequent along the nine miles. Longtime natives, used to seeing decades of dreamers come and go, top their cynicism with that age-old conclusion, "Only in El Paso." Many of them share this attitude while they brace for Y2K. I go back to my mother's house where I am staying and she hands me a note from David Acosta, a graduate student at UTEP. He has tracked me down because he is building a Web site about the dozens of published Chicano writers who were born in El Paso and live elsewhere. He wants me to give him a list of my latest books, details about my awards and teaching career, and comments about why so many successful Mexican American writers, native to the border, have fled their hometown and made it elsewhere. He leaves his e-mail address on the note. I decide to wait until I get back to Minnesota before I respond. There is plenty of time to think about his questions. I want to make sure I get back before Gopher fans flood the Minneapolis airport. I don't want to witness the defeated hordes stepping off their hot plane wearing sombreros and cowboy boots that pinch their feet as they try to erase dazed looks from spending a disappointing time in a desert that didn't even notice they were there.

El Mercado

Aztec and Mayan statues with long faces. Marionettes with sombreros on twisted strings. T-shirts that say "motherfucker" in Spanish. Packs of Horseshit cigarettes. Elvis on black velvet paintings. Crucifixes of a bleeding Christ in sizes from two inches to three feet. Posters of Oscar de la Hoya, Madonna, Selena, Pancho Villa, Subcommander Marcos, and the late Princess Diana of England. Leather purses. Belts. Cowboy boots. Sandals. Jewelry promoted as Indian original with factory markings all over it. Knives. Machetes. Switchblades. Swiss Army knives at very low prices. Rosaries of every color and bead size. Rosaries that glow in the dark. T-shirts with rosary beads printed on them. Lacquered bullhorns. Maracas. Bongo drums. Wooden flutes. Indian headdresses, not Aztec or Mayan, but North American Plains Indian war bonnets sold only in Mexico. Plastic lizards and plastic turtles. Rubber snakes and rubber bats. Mass produced pottery of every size and design, dozens of the pots sitting cracked amid rows and rows of pottery. Mass produced, circular Aztec calendars made out of clay, plastic, glass, or woven straw, their codex patterns forming symbols of every size and possible interpretation. A mean-looking vendor arguing with a turista over the price of a piñata of a donkey, the vendor speaking in bad English and the turista in bad Spanish. African masks with a Mexican twist. Piñatas of Mexican wrestlers. One mask with only one eye in the middle of the forehead. Mexican flags of every size stuck into styrofoam holders; a couple of turistas buying a foot-long flag to wave up and down the aisles. El Diablo masks in red clay with sucking lips and glowing horns. Angel masks on which the blissful plastic face is painted a pale tone, lighter than human, with plastic halos of chicken wire tied at the top of each mask. Snow globes full of water and Christmas scenes; a turista shaking one to watch the snow fall off a sexy woman Santa, her naked body revealed after the snow settles inside the globe. Headbands and hairpins. Cases of lipstick in every color imaginable, including black, blue, and green. Kachinas from New Mexico of every deity. Tiny metal statues of Spanish conquistadores in every fighting stance imaginable, swords, lances, and shields held high. A music box that opens to a fat bandit dropping his pants and taking a shit as the music begins, the turd retreating back up his ass when the box is closed. Mexican flags on soda straws. Mexican flags on long toothpicks. Mexican flag underwear for men and women, the boxer shorts and huge bras allowing ample room for several flag patterns. Mexican flag T-shirts. La Virgen de Guadalupe T-shirts. Zapatista T-shirts showing a band of armed and black-masked guerillas pointing M-16s, their grins shining through their masks. Tiny plastic water guns on a revolving rack. Bibles in Spanish of every size imaginable; an old woman sitting behind the Bible counter reading a police detective magazine whose cover shows the blud-geoned body of a naked woman. Bamboo bird cages. Traditional chess sets next to sets whose playing pieces are naked women, pigs and cows, cow-boy boots (with the king and queen represented by larger, shinier boots), science-fiction-type globes and space-alien monsters, geometric shapes, and what look like heads of gringo men and women. Scorpions of every size preserved in amber glass. Rattlesnakes of every size and color coiled and preserved in glass and several dried and mounted on sticks. Spanish swords. Pocket mirrors. Full-length floor mirrors. Boxes of razor blades, a few spilled across glass counters and display cases, a few with worn and rusty edges. Black velvet paintings of a blonde who looks like either Madonna or Marilyn Monroe, depending on the angle of light filtering down through the broken windows two stories above the main mercado floor. Three or four federal-looking policemen watching the narrow aisles of merchandise and turistas from second-floor balconies. Watermelons. Huge apples and apricots and mounds of lemons and limes drawing clouds of flies; several sliced oranges sitting in buckets of ice drawing more flies. Pocket radios. A few cell phones sitting in torn open boxes, the instructions missing, some of the instruments battered as if they have been used many times. Beepers of every size, all of them made to fit into coat or pants pockets. Black velvet paintings of Pancho Villa. Pocket cassette players. Watches of every size and color. Metates for grinding masa. Painted gourds adorned with Aztec warriors in dance and heated battle. Stacks of hot corn and flour tortillas and hotter chile at the food stands. Cokes and Pepsis in bottles packed in ice inside open freezers. Bras and girdles of various colors wrapped in plastic; dozens of pairs of women's underwear stacked in an overflowing pile on a counter, several pairs fallen on the concrete floor, dirty footprints of turistas branding the bright pink and yellow material. Huge glass jars of lemonade, clusters of lemons floating in the cloudy water. Huge glass jars of limeade, clusters of limes floating in the cloudy water, one jar containing a wristwatch that has fallen to the bottom of the jar, its hands stopped at 12:03, several slices of limes obscuring it from the young guy calling out to the turistas to stop and buy some "limonada!" Donald Duck dolls in sombreros and bandoliers. Mickey Mouse in purple and pink zoot suits. Minnie Mouse in street-walker leather. Aztec codices made of clay, plastic, wood, and colored tiles. Boxes of Aztec-brand condoms, the smiling face of a plumed warrior decorating the foil. Gourds painted in a variety of colors. Retablos, silver bracelets, hammocks, lacquered wooden trays, copal animals, many of them of unknown species. Packets of Lotería playing cards. Miniature color photos of John Wayne, Lyndon Johnson, John F. Kennedy, and Ronald Reagan mounted in bright gold lockets, each one in its own necklace. Black velvet paintings of La Virgen de Guadalupe. Vendors smoking, vendors sleeping behind their counters, vendors counting coins, vendors shouting to each other, vendors silently watching turistas walk by without buying. Mouse traps for one nickel. Giant cans of jalapeños, huge cans of red chile sauce, small cans of tamales for those who prefer them over the real thing. Empty straw baskets with lids to store freshly made tortillas. Quartz Aztec gods in glass cases from one inch to one foot tall. Pan dulce of every flavor, shape, and sweetness; a number of empty racks attracting flies and tiny black bugs that cling to the sugar left on the metal trays. Black velvet paintings of Jesus Christ. Bags of glowing marbles of every color. Posters of burros, donkeys, and monkeys staring into the camera, the posters consisting of nothing but burros, donkeys, and monkeys staring into the camera. One boy chasing loose marbles across the cement aisle as the bag in his hands tears and marbles bounce away. Acoustic guitars and basses hanging on wooden rafters above the narrow aisles. Beautiful hand-carved violins and sextos. Mestizo shirts and blouses of all sizes and patterns. Ceramic suns painted with various faces and expressions. Beaded iguanas, lizards, spiders, and turtles. Tiger masks. Coyote masks. Donkey masks. Monkey masks. Spiderman masks. Batman and Robin masks. Zorro masks. Three Richard Nixon masks, probably collectors' items. Metal fly swatters for one dime. Serapes and blankets. One steaming kitchen counter selling stacks of Chinese egg rolls and nothing else. Cigarette lighters with tigers, pandas, dragons, and nude women emblazoned into the metal. Vendors swatting flies on pans of meat and mangos. Turistas eating dripping burritos in the aisles. Dog collars made of elastic. A rack of bicycles, perhaps one dozen, most of them hanging with flat tires, twisted handle bars, and rusted metal bodies, only two of them with seats for the biker. Rosaries, most of them containing black beads, a few of white or sky blue. Black velvet paintings of Lyndon Johnson. Tablecloths of every imaginable design and color, the ones with Mexican wrestler patterns and Zapatistas in black masks standing out. Huge baskets of fresh jalapeños, corn, beans, rice, and tomatoes, and racks of sizzling goat meat, frying and filling the place with their smell. Spanish conquistador helmets for the kids. Finger mazes with openings for one left and one right finger that lock without letting go. Black velvet paintings of John F. Kennedy. Bullfighter capes, worn by a fat vendor with his long hair tied back in a ponytail, the gap of his missing teeth highlighting his glee at swirling the crimson capes over his shoulders and across the aisles. Hot and smoking pans of tripas, cesos, and menudo. Packs of popsicle sticks for ice cream cart vendors. Packs of paper cups for raspa and snowcone vendors. Plastic dolls of hairless Tepezcuintles dogs, at one time a part of the diet of ancient Mexicans. A small Indian girl standing behind a counter watching the turistas going by, her bare feet black with dirt, her torn yellow dress stained with every color imaginable, her vivid, dark eyes staring at each passing person as snot drips down her nose. Plaster of Paris statues of black bulls with horns. Plaster of Paris statues of Cantinflas, Godzilla, Popeye the Sailor Man, Spider Man, Zorro, and a black, twisted thing that tries to pass as Darth Vader. Brightly colored, barbed short spears, the kind bullfighters embed in the shoulders of bulls to wear them down with slow bleeding. Car batteries, new and used, the acid eating through the cardboard boxes onto the concrete floor. Flashlights of every size and color. Boxes and boxes of flashlight batteries of every size. Day of the Dead skeleton puppets, key rings, necklaces. Walls of brightly colored blankets, their rainbow colors blending together; two or three vendors strolling up and down the hanging display, running their hands over the fine material. Racks of traditional women's clothing from the interior of Mexico, including Huipil sleeveless tunics, Quechquemitl shoulder capes, and dozens of enredos, those wraparound skirts women wore in the past that are rarely seen along the border today; this part of the mercado one of the emptiest, though its line of beautiful clothing makes it one of the more attractive. Skull cigarette ashtrays, skull tattooed drinking glasses, candy and bread skulls, skeleton underwear of every size, even a small shelf against the back of one booth containing packs of condoms wrapped in black foil with images of skeletons on the wrappers— a warning of death if you don't wear one or what might happen if you do? Mountains of corn husks for tamales, bags of flour for making tortillas, huge chunks of pork rinds with pieces of meat and fat still on them. Pornographic playing cards of women, pornographic playing cards of men. Barbie dolls with brown skin and fruit baskets on their heads. Beggars at every arched doorway into El Mercado begging for anything. Federal police standing by the parking meters, guns in their belts, watching old men who wait for the turistas to return and give them one dollar for keeping roving kids away from their cars. One drunk beggar, dark skinned, with a three-day-old beard and wet hair, crawling between cars, the new T-shirt he wears emblazoned with a colorful image of Emiliano Zapata, the legendary hero's huge moustache and revolver pointing straight at the startled turista who can't find his car.

Part Two

The General on the Border

Escaped Prisoner Enjoys His Liberty

The political refugees fraternity of El Paso has received a notable recruit, Francisco "Pancho" Villa, erstwhile bandit rebel, ex-insurrecto
and jail breaker. Pancho "escaped" a week ago from the penitentiary
in Mexico City and has arrived in El Paso in fine fettle with plenty of
dinero. Dressed as a Spanish bullfighter or priest, Villa put in his
appearance Saturday afternoon in El Paso. He wore a hard hat and a
long black cape, beneath which, rumor has it, is cutlery and artillery
both heavy and light. He had an enjoyable day Sunday. He rode

around with his young wife who accompanied him. He is charged by Mexican General Huerta with looting. The Consul in El Paso did not apprehend him.

—*El Paso Herald,* January 13, 1913

Villa Buys Second Car; Licence Is Issued Here
Revolutions seem profitable. Pancho Villa has two automobiles registered in the county clerk's office. No. 1896 was the number taken out for Villa for a seven-passenger Packard car Tuesday afternoon. On November 17 the county clerk issued No. 1837 to Villa for a five-passenger Hudson car. Villa's family at present is living at 610 South Oregon Street in El Paso.

—*El Paso Herald,* December 17, 1913

Villa Donates $1,000 to Buy Clothes for Families of Federals
General Pancho Villa gave $1,000 Tuesday to a local charity organization to purchase clothes for women and children in the Mexican Federal prison camp at Fort Bliss, Texas. It is said that the organization appealed to the Huerta consul in El Paso for funds to alleviate the sufferings of the prisoners but were turned down by the Mexican president's representatives.

—*El Paso Herald,* February 3, 1914

Doctor Interviews Pancho Villa
Washington, D.C.—"Just had an interview with Villa. He wishes to salute you affectionately and says you need have no anxiety." This was the message delivered today to General Hugh H. Scott, assistant chief of staff of the army, from Doctor Carlos E. Rusk of El Paso. General Scott had known Villa for some time, the two having faced each other across the Rio Grande for many weeks at El Paso and Juárez.

—*El Paso Herald,* April 24, 1914

It is June 5, Pancho Villa's birthday, and I find his death mask in the new El Paso Museum of History. Upon closer inspection of the strange object in the glass case, I notice the plaster face is turned upside down, his nose pressed to the bottom of the locked cabinet, the bloated features of the dead Mexican hero staring at me from a faded photograph next to the mold. The sign says this is the death mask, but after seeing what the curator of the Pancho Villa Museum in Columbus, New Mexico, claims is the actual death mask, I conclude this one is only the round mold that formed a face. One year earlier, in a tiny railroad station in the only U.S. town invaded by a foreign army in the twentieth century, I listened to Martha Billings, the curator, say, "Yes, ladies and gentlemen. Columbus is the lucky owner of one of only five death masks of Pancho Villa. We are very proud to have it."

The dead man in the El Paso museum photograph doesn't look like the dead man whose bright pink cheeks and ruby red lips adorn the glass case in Martha's depot, even though the features in the photograph look real compared to the Columbus mask that has been painted in a creepy color. Why does the label in El Paso say it is a death mask, and why is the face on the mold turned away from museum visitors? I ponder this mystery about Doroteo Arango Francisco "Pancho" Villa on his birthday. I showed up at the new museum unaware this was the date of his birth until I read the brochures in the museum. This puzzle over grisly remains of the General is part of the legends and contradictions of the U.S.–Mexican border. To many, Pancho Villa is the ultimate Mexican stereotype, with huge sombrero, thick moustache, and bandoliers loaded with bullets crossing his chest. He is the bad guy who killed hundreds of men with guns, knives, and bare hands, while he raped countless American and Mexican women and took eight wives over his lifetime. How about the revolutionary leader who freed thousands of people from tyranny, was governor of the state of Chihuahua, led the biggest armies during the Mexican Revolution, and almost became president of Mexico? Villa was a legend when he was assassinated in Parral, Mexico, on July 20, 1923—three years after the revolution ended. To this day, Mexicans embrace the good and bad myths about him, while Americans still don't know who the real Pancho Villa was or what kind of place to give him within border culture. The two contradictory death masks I've seen remind me of a larger mystery: the whereabouts of his head. Rumors persist that in 1926, grave robbers dug up his body in Parral and stole his skull. Years later, the Mexican government wanted Villa's body moved to Mexico City, but further rumors say the mayor of Parral substituted another body that was sent instead. In 1966 the

Mexican Senate officially recognized Villa as a hero of the revolution and approved the writing of his name on gold letters on the walls of the Chamber of Deputies. He is now buried in a Hall of Heroes in Mexico City.

I am here to experience a different approach to Villa's legend—the one created by heritage tourism. By riding on the Border Jumper trolley over sixty miles of barren desert to Columbus, I discovered the General and his invasion of the United States is relived over and over in a tiny, ramshackle town that thrives on his legend. Pancho Villa is essential to the tourist trade in the El Paso area. The mystery of two different death masks representing the same man fits the way border economic dreamers have rearranged the past for the best dollar yield, taking a region rich in historical significance and squeezing as many fabricated myths out of it as possible.

When I bought my tour ticket at the El Paso Convention Center, I already knew a great deal about the Columbus raid and Villa's presence at the battle, which has been long debated by historians. Around four A.M. on March 9, 1916, two hundred Villistas crossed the border at Palomas and attacked the six-hundred-man U.S. Army garrison at Camp Furlong in Columbus. The Villa detachment was mostly made up of his elite Dorado guard, veterans of years of fighting. Fifteen U.S. soldiers were killed and several buildings in the town were burned by Villa's men. Conflicting reports on the number of Villistas killed by the Americans have ranged from sixty to eighty. Town people who witnessed the raid claimed that more than a hundred Mexicans were found in the street in the morning daylight, then thrown into a huge pile and burned. Eleven of Villa's men, including two boys, twelve and sixteen, were captured. One boy, Jesús Piaz, had his left leg amputated in a Deming hospital after a U.S. bullet hit him. Six other prisoners were hanged in Santa Fe and Deming a few weeks after a hasty trial. Villa stayed with a small group of his men south of the border and watched the battle from there.

The Villistas held no territory and may have taken supplies and horses from the town, but they vanished into the desert in less than one hour after setting fire to several buildings. Historians and Villa mythmakers claim the attack was in retaliation for an arms deal gone sour. This is the Mexican view—a popular hero and general fighting the evil dictatorship of Porfirio Díaz and desperate for help, is swindled by greedy American arms dealers and comes for revenge. The Mexican side adds that arms merchant Sam Ravel sold movie blanks instead of real bullets to Villa's army. Of course, Ravel was not in Columbus the night of the raid. American popular opinion says the raid was an expression of Villa's frustration with the fact that the United States was backing Venustiano Carranza, one of several Mexican leaders who fought over the presidency during the long years of the Mexican Revolution. Other theories about the raid say American businessmen, eager for U.S. intervention to capture fertile ranchland for their profit, paid Villa to attack. John Reed, the famous expatriate writer and leftist, accepted this theory in his writings about the revolution.

As a result of the Columbus attack, a call to arms was issued by the Americans, who sent a large army, commanded by General John J. Pershing, into northern Mexico to capture Villa. The rallying cry came in an assortment of ways. In April 1916, one month after the Columbus battle, a film titled *Villa Dead or Alive* was released by the Eagle Films Company. Its advertising boldly cried:

> That's what President Woodrow Wilson said, and that's what we are going to do.
> Is the United States prepared?
> Go and see Uncle Sam's troops in action.
> See your flag cross the border to punish those who have insulted it.

Advertising for another film, *Following the Flag in Mexico*, produced by the Feinberg Amusement Corporation, announced: "Villa at any cost. $20,000 reward, dead or alive. Mexican bandit bands in action." General Pershing staged a press conference in Columbus before his expedition went after Villa, claiming the bandit and his men would be rounded up within days. Among the hundreds of photographs taken of Pershing's troops and newly invented armored vehicles and machine guns are several shots of American women who made up the traveling brothel Pershing brought along for his troops. Perhaps they were afraid they might really catch something if they got too close to the sparse Mexican population of northern Chihuahua.

Villa eluded Pershing for more than six months; his men reportedly followed the posse around and hid behind huge clouds of dust the Americans kicked up with their mule trains and motorized vehicles. The expedition was not a complete waste, because the U.S. troops got the chance to test new weapons against invisible targets in the desert, evaluating their firepower as they prepared to enter World War I. There is a legend that says Villa, disguised as a peasant, actually walked into a U.S. Army camp one day and stood next to Pershing, who failed to recognize him, though they had met before in El Paso. Villa trusted no one, so he carried out his own spying operations. What was clear to him, his followers, and his enemies was that the Columbus raid gave new life to his cause against Díaz and Francisco Madero, a Villa rival with his own army who became president after Díaz was assassinated during the war.

Eastern Firm Writes General Pershing Asking for Body of Villa

A Dyersburg, Tennessee, firm that advertises that it handles "undertaking furniture, carpets, matting, and window shades," has written General Pershing, asking for Villa's body if he is killed. The firm says it would like to embalm the body and keep it on display.

—*El Paso Herald,* March 28, 1916

The Face of a Brutal Killer, Not a Hero, Is Revealed

The picture on the left side is a snapshot showing the brutal, sensual mouth and jaw, the small cruel eyes and the general bestial appearance of the real Villa. On the right is a studio picture of Villa in his uniform as Constitutionalist officer and the pride of many Mexicans fighting in the revolution. Below, Villa is seen in the midst of some of his horsemen at a wayside camp.

—*El Paso Herald,* April 1, 1916

Mexicans Say Villa Slain; Troops Hunt Body

Mexicans of northern Chihuahua are well disposed toward the American army and many of them profess bitter enmity against Francisco Villa. General Pershing has received renewed reports that Villa is dead and buried. While the reports are under investigation, the hunt for Villistas is proceeding with renewed vigor with the arrival of General Pershing at the front.

—*El Paso Herald,* April 11, 1916

If Villa Is Dead, He Will Be Buried Nearby

Pancho Villa, one time czar of more than half of Mexico, will be buried in the potter's field in Juárez, if he is dead and if his body is recovered and brought to Juárez. The body of Villa is reported as being brought overland from Francisco de Borja to Cusihuiriachic, a distance of some 30 miles, and the report is that it will arrive there sometime today.

—*El Paso Herald,* April 17, 1916

Pancho Villa Alive, with and without His Leg,
Seen from Raleigh to Pasadena

When Mrs. Rose Cohn of Los Angeles, California, gave a curious American public the word that she recently saw Pancho Villa seated in a large black motor car and that she knew it was Villa, because she had seen him on numerous occasions while doing Red Cross work in Mexico, it developed a wave of sightings across the U.S. Where is Villa?

—*El Paso Herald,* April 24, 1916

Hesitating to buy my ticket to Columbus, I walk around the El Paso Convention Center. Two minibuses, decorated to resemble turn-of-the-century trolley cars and carrying signs that say El Paso Trolley Company, are parked curbside before the enormous concrete building. Decades ago, the convention center became an El Paso landmark after its roof was designed to resemble a sombrero. The old Greyhound bus station, once located across from the center, is now the brand new El Paso Museum of Art. Dozens of construction barricades line the streets around the museum and San Jacinto Plaza to the east. I want to buy my ticket for the Villa ride. The twelve-dollar ticket is cheap compared to many tourist attractions, but the sight of the silly-looking buses and the construction force me to cross the street instead. I'm hungry, having skipped breakfast, but the tour includes a Mexican meal in the Pink Restaurant in Palomas as part of the package. It was listed in the newspaper ad in the Sunday *El Paso Times,* where the announcement of a guided tour to Columbus had caught me by surprise. I had planned to drive there alone, taking the highway to Las Cruces, then west to Deming before heading south to Columbus—a loop of 180 miles and three hours. The newspaper ad boasted a one-hour ride over the new Highway 9, its two-lane blacktop separated from the international border fence by a few yards, paralleling it all the way to Columbus, now only sixty miles due west from Santa Teresa in the Upper Valley.

As I scan the surrounding mess of dump trucks, tractors, and men wearing hard hats, I am amazed at the massive transformation of the city. It is no longer the downtown of my childhood or the ancient center of an old western town with crumbling buildings. El Paso is being redone in concrete, though much of downtown and the people who appear there every day make it look like Juárez. I stroll through a barricaded block of a half-finished office building and pass a row of turquoise-colored portable toilets, set there for the construction crews and used by homeless, begging individuals in the area. Two old Tewa Indian women with decimated features lean against a closed toilet door and a small boy calls out to one of them from inside. Most of the toilet doors are covered in graffiti, but I can read only one message sprayed in bright orange letters: "Cristo Viene Pronto." Christ Comes Soon. I stop and stare at the announcement as a jackhammer starts a few yards away and the shouts of workmen are drowned out. The explosion of sound convinces me to go to the convention center and buy my ticket. The Indian women watch me pass, and one of them opens the toilet door to let the boy out. I can't be as hungry as they appear to be and I give each one a dollar. Downtown El Paso looks hungry, making me feel as if I never spent twenty-five years of my life here.

Three people stand ahead of me to buy tickets to Columbus. The tiny office of the El Paso Trolley Company contains a counter with two busy women behind it. The older woman is shouting orders to the younger one and laughing at the same time.

"Yeah, it's gonna be a hot one today," she smiles at the first person in line, a young African American woman, "but you know the border is always hot!"

"We've got plenty of seats, sir," she assures an older man who is next. "We supply soft drinks and bottles of water. Any extra liquids and you're on your own!" She laughs at this, bends over her computer cash register and punches the keyboard. "Ole Martha at the museum in Columbus will tell you all about our friend Pancho," she says to the old man in answer to something he whispers to her. "He's waiting for us there every time."

The woman in front of me is a Mexican who must be in her late sixties. Her sleek figure is clothed in tight black pants and a thin tank top, an unusual style for a Mexican woman of her age. A heavy cloud of perfume moves past me as I stand behind this woman. Her long black hair is tied in a pony tail, and huge silver earrings jangle as she pays for her ticket. She asks the loud cashier about the Border Jumper tour to Juárez.

"Our most popular ride," the cashier answers. "We go twice a month, but Columbus takes all day. We won't be back until late this afternoon." She takes the woman's money as I inspect one of the most attractive older women I have ever seen. She takes her ticket, doesn't notice I am there, and bumps into me when she steps back.

"Aye! Con permiso," she whispers to me.

I back off as her brown, sandaled foot removes itself from my foot. It makes me wonder what the day is going to be like as I buy my ticket. The loud woman behind the counter is our tour guide. Her name tag reads Kay Johnson, El Paso Trolley Company. She gives orders to her employee, grabs a baseball cap, and disappears into a back room. I follow the three others outside, where we are joined by ten people who already have tickets, two Mexicans and one other African American among them. The rest of the group stand by the buses, their sunglasses, hats, and freshly pressed shorts and golf shirts shining in the morning sun.

We board what turn out to be minivans, and I grab a seat in the back row by the window. Kay takes our tickets and checks us off a list. "Where is Al?" she mutters to herself, looking for her driver. Al comes running out of the office and hops on board to warm up the engine. There is plenty of room for everybody, and no one sits with me. Couples and lone individuals settle in and remove hats, laughing and shuffling camera bags as Kay shuts the doors.

Al takes Paisano Drive, south of the convention center, and heads north. I settle back as we pass familiar parts of town and go by the last place where I lived in El Paso, a tiny house torn down years ago. The site, twenty yards from the Rio Grande, is now paved over with an international monument on the history of El Paso del Norte. The marker has been erected on the exact spot where my house stood and is adorned with flags from several countries that had a role in the cycle of conquest—Spain, France, Mexico, and the United States. As the bus enters traffic on Paisano, I want to get off; I realize this is the first time I am not in control of my explorations. I have always been the one to decide where to go, which road to take, which obscure spot to stop at, and how long to wander the desert. I stare at the ancient smoke-stacks of the Asarco Chemical Plant as we pick up speed and leave the ugly factory behind. My apprehension over joining this tour rises, then casually fades when I admit to myself that a lone drive to Columbus would not give me a chance to find out what kind of people today are curious about Pancho Villa. Fourteen people know enough to hop on board. I wonder how profitable these tours are for Kay Johnson.

"Good morning, everybody!" her shrill voices cuts into my thoughts as it blares over the loudspeaker. Kay is sitting in front of the bus facing her passengers, a microphone stuck close to her mouth. Her curly blonde hair, heavy makeup, and navy blue shirt with her trolley logo make her look like a Disneyland ride operator.

"It's a beautiful day for Pancho Villa!" she chortles and sends feedback screaming through our ears. Two people cover theirs as she turns down the volume on the dashboard. "Sorry. Is that better?" Her smooth voice is perfect over the speakers.

"Welcome to the Columbus ride. We are in our third year of taking people to Columbus, New Mexico, site of the famous invasion led by that crazy Pancho Villa. This is becoming one of our best adventures. I also want to let you know we are planning tours to Mesilla, New Mexico, and Carlsbad Caverns. Who can tell me about Pancho Villa?"

I can't believe this and hunker down on my seat as two elderly women, riding together, raise their hands. "Yes! Yes!" Kay cries. "Tell us your names."

"My name is Vinnie Portland, and this is my friend Sarah. Pancho Villa was the Mexican villain who stole from the Americans and fought the Mexican government. He had a house in El Paso, you know," Vinnie states.

"He had many houses and many women," Kay corrects her. "He was deranged and many people don't know what to think of him. How many of you think he was a great hero? Raise your hands. Who knows why he was so crazy?"

I look out the window as Al turns onto the freeway and leaves Paisano and the river behind. Four people raise their hands, then quickly put them down.

"How many of you think he was a revolutionary terrorist and should have been hung by the U.S. Army?"

Six people, including Vinnie and Sarah, raise their hands and cheer.

"Well," Kay says and stands up. She wraps an arm around a safety rail and begins, "Pancho Villa and the myths about him are part of our history. We are passing out this short bio on him. He was famous, but he was deranged and killed many people. Lots of people from Mexico hated him. We don't even know if he was at Columbus the day of the raid. Some people say he was right here in El Paso. Others say he was in Mexico City. But, when we get to Columbus, you will see Pancho and his men got quite a response from the Americans."

I shake my head at her comments. It is obvious Kay has her routine down and must repeat this stuff on every ride, filling her clients with erroneous information about Villa. There are military documents and eyewitness accounts that prove his presence in the Columbus area that morning. Deranged? I want to laugh aloud, but Kay starts screaming over the speaker again.

"It's just over an hour to Columbus over Highway 9. We have soft drinks and water we will pass out shortly. Don't forget to stay together. It's going to be a great day, so I want to begin by having all of you introduce yourselves."

Just what I need. We go around and I say my name and nothing else. Three people are from other parts of Texas and three from Juárez, including the Mexican woman named Elsa who stepped on my foot. The rest are El Pasoans. I am surprised at this, assuming these tours drew a majority of participants from out of town. Many locals I have questioned about Villa in the past had not even heard of the town of Columbus. One middle-aged woman sits back and pulls out her knitting bag! An elderly African American woman who has been sitting quietly across from me introduces herself as Molly Sanders and tells us her grandfather was a Buffalo Soldier stationed at Fort Bliss in El Paso during the Mexican Revolution. She says he never went to Columbus but remembered her grandfather Roy talk about his adventures with Pershing's army as it chased Villa all over northern Mexico.

After the introductions, the group settles down and Kay spares us further use of the microphone. She is too busy telling Al where to turn to get to Santa Teresa and the new highway and passing out sodas to everybody, though it is still morning. When I lived here in the early seventies, Santa Teresa had just been built as a golf course, about twenty miles north of El Paso. Now it was a growing town in itself, had its own airport, and was located next to the newest international border crossing, the United States and Mexico having opened it recently to try to handle the growing border traffic and industrial trade.

Al gets lost in Santa Teresa for a few minutes, does a U-turn, then heads in the right direction. We pass a Border Patrol station that didn't exist years ago. Highway 9 begins where Santa Teresa ends and is a flat, straight shot across one of the most desolate parts of New Mexico. The highway runs past the Aden Lava Flow and Kilbourne Hole, ancient lava beds and old volcanoes that used to be gathering spots for teenagers when I was in high school. Driving out to them years ago was a big thrill because there was nothing but dirt roads, rattlesnakes, and the sheer desert night. The new highway speeds past the black formations and connects what used to be wild desert to the uncontrolled growth of the area. It also runs past long rows of maquiladoras, factories that U.S. companies have built in Mexico. Their ugly metal buildings and warehouses line the international boundary line to my left, only fifty yards from the border. We pass at least three miles of nothing but factory buildings.

The enormous Chihuahuan Desert is breathtaking in the morning. I sip on a Diet Coke and take in a landscape that is menacing and beautiful at once. To my right, the West Potrillo Mountains rise in bare walls of red rock, their broken cliffs and low canyons fading into distant miles of yucca and mesquite. There are no roads, no water, and no signs of life for miles. I close my eyes and hope Kay doesn't start again. A few low conversations from the others compete with the smooth rolling pace of the van. People look out their windows or contemplate nothing as we head west. To my left, the tightly wound and closed border fence lines the horizon, long sections of it extending beyond my sight. I turn to my right in time to catch two eagles soaring in the distance, where the blue sky falls into a deeper blue.

Then I notice the white poles. Every hundred yards, their steel rises at least fifty feet into the air. I have only an instant in the speeding bus to spot the cameras mounted at the tops of the poles. Someone beats me to asking Kay about them. She breaks her silence. "Border Patrol cameras and sensors line the border from here past Columbus. Those are cameras, folks. Smile." No one says anything because I bet no one cares about such things. One camera every hundred yards and sensors buried in between each. I can't calculate how many hundred yards in one mile times the sixty miles to Columbus. I can't see if the cameras are pointed north and south because we are going too fast. I wonder where the control center for such a massive network is located and who watches all those screens. The media have done stories about a supposedly secret, high-tech center at Fort Bliss in El Paso. It is one of the most sophisticated eavesdropping operations in North America and part of the U.S. militarization of the border. I spot more eagles as I think about U.S. attempts to stop illegal immigration and drug trafficking and wind up counting five huge birds before we reach Columbus. Sandy washes and faraway mountains break the horizon, clusters of enormous yucca looking like foot soldiers of an invading army, though the cameras and border fence make me imagine the real people who cross. Why would anyone choose this stark, threatening area as a place to enter the United States? What was Villa thinking when he chose Columbus? I focus on a tiny white speck in the western sky, thinking it is another eagle, but its brightness tells me it is not. I decide it is a small plane, but the white dot seems to stay in the same spot. It is growing as we get closer.

Kay's electric voice makes me jump. "We are about twenty miles from Columbus. Is everybody awake? Any more water or sodas before we get there? There are bathrooms in the museum. We are going to play a little game before we get to Columbus. It's called the oldest penny. Whoever can find the penny with the oldest date on it gets our new El Paso Trolley Company travel bag! Look at your pennies."

There is a small commotion, but I don't participate. Elsa wins with her 1951 penny, beating out a 1966 coin by Jimmy, an elderly man. Kay is about to sit back down when the old man points to the growing white thing in the sky.

"What is that?" Jimmy asks.

Kay barely turns, knowing what he means. "Oh, yes. Ladies and gentlemen, one of the modern characteristics of Columbus, New Mexico, is its proud balloon. When we get closer, you can see it better. The U.S. Drug Enforcement Agency has tethered a drug balloon in Columbus for many years. It is a radar device to track low-flying drug-smuggling planes from Mexico. I think it rises about two hundred feet in the sky. Three years ago, a small plane crashed near the town and they busted some guy with tons of marijuana. Ha! Ha! Ha! Does anyone know if Pancho Villa smoked drugs?"

I close my eyes, anxious to pull into Columbus. When I open them, we have rounded one of the few curves on the highway and slow down as one of the most decrepit settlements I have ever seen comes into view. A black water tower rises at the edge of town, its rusting letters barely spelling "Welcome to Columbus, New Mexico."

Another of Villa's Ex-Friends Reveals Bandits True Colors
The following denunciation from Chocano John W. Roberts, who has ridden with Villa in his car, eaten with him in his camp, and been very close in every way, tells of the leader's true character. "When a savage animal of the wilds is cornered, he loses all control of his senses and will fight anything and everything that comes near him. General Francisco Villa today is a savage animal at bay."
—*El Paso Herald,* September 15, 1916

Villa Is Now at Santa Rosalía, Threatens to Kill Americans
"Pancho" Villa is now in Santa Rosalía, or was a week ago. He declares that "all American filibusters" must get out of Mexico or he will kill them. He has locked up the women of the best families of Santa Rosalía and has confiscated their homes and furnitures. He has seized all the money in the place and there is not $500 in circulation in the city. He has declared he will kill every American that crosses into Mexico.
—*El Paso Herald,* September 23, 1916

Villa to Sign with Circus
A circus tent. Silence. The fluttering of Mexican flags. Then suddenly "La Paloma" music by the circus band. The traditional blaring of trumpets and then in the center ring, waving his hat to those who gaze upon him, appears a swarthy, heavyset man with teeth and eyes that shine, Pancho Villa of Mexico, who is joining the largest circus in Mexico.
—*El Paso Herald,* October 23, 1916

Pancho Villa Elementary. Pancho Villa Middle School. Pancho Villa Historical Museum. Pancho Villa State Park. It seems the only building not named after Villa is Betty's Place, the only bed and breakfast in Columbus.

The doors to the small, pink adobe building are shut and curtained as we slowly pass by. In the summer of 2000, the population of Columbus is eight hundred citizens and one enormous balloon floating above the town. Trailer homes dot the dirt streets, junked cars rust in fields, dogs bark behind fences, and not a soul is in sight. Every low wooden hut and old brick dwelling give the feeling of being abandoned. Where is everybody? The settlement sits in a valley surrounded by low hills and looks out of place. I find out later that most of the people who live in town work in Deming, about forty miles to the north. The Pancho Villa Historical Museum, run by the Columbus Historical Society, is actually the old train stop and one of the tiniest stations I have ever seen. Al parks the bus in front and I get a glimpse behind the building of the railroad tracks that disappear to the west. The station is painted a dull army yellow, like the old barracks at Fort Bliss. I wait for Kay to blare instructions over the speaker, but she waves everybody off the van with a big smile, jumping excitedly off the bus first. The fourteen of us file out behind her and step into the museum.

"Hi, everybody! Welcome to Columbus, New Mexico, site of the famous raid by Pancho Villa and one of the greatest victories by the U.S. Army!" This voice belongs to Martha Billings, director of the Historical Society and hostess of the museum. "Come on in and look around. Take your time. There is a lot to look at."

She is a tall woman with gray hair and a rough, western demeanor. She sets a clipboard down on the front counter and watches each of us pass into the main exhibit room, which is barely larger than the van we rode in. Black-and-white army photos line the walls, along with medals, badges, military flags of every kind, maps of New Mexico and old Mexico, realistic charcoal sketches of U.S. soldiers in the early twentieth century, and caricatures of banditos—exaggerated drawings of the bad guys, most of them looking like Villa, their menacing expressions decorated with thick moustaches, rifles and guns in hand. One yellowing drawing depicts Mexicans running in terror from the Americans who chase them down on horses. The first photograph to really catch my attention shows several Mexicans hanging from gallows in Deming.

Ancient glass and wood cabinets in the crowded room are filled with guns, rifles, bullets, bandoliers, boots, belts, knives, and every conceivable kind of hat, bandana, and holster worn by U.S. and Mexican troops almost one hundred years ago. A larger case holds swords, complete uniforms, even old irons for pressing them, and several women's dresses. The labels claim the outfits belonged to the brave wives and widows of veterans of the Villa attack. Kay and Martha talk quietly by the front door as our band of tourists squeezes into the room to inspect the antique treasures of an event left out of American history books. Headlines from crumbling El Paso and New Mexico newspapers are framed on the walls, several detailing the long years of the Mexican Revolution, with most of them focusing on the Columbus raid. I count twelve U.S. flags of different sizes on the walls without a single Mexican flag in sight.

Elsa and Jimmy wander next to me and the three of us look down at a display that has caught our attention. The few color photographs in the place are mounted above a glass cabinet and show the street corner in Parral where Villa and six of his men were ambushed and killed. The street is empty, without Villa's automobile or bullet holes in the walls. Later, in El Paso, I will stumble upon actual photographs of the assassination. These captions tell how Villa and his men received more than a hundred bullets, Villa taking sixteen hits himself. The shooters are described as opponents of Villa's political forces, but the facts emerging over the years have proven the men who killed him were hired by a local businessman who discovered his wife had been sleeping with the General.

I wonder what the tie between the raid in 1916 and the 1923 killing might be, until I peer through the dusty glass and meet the death mask of Villa. I recoil for a second, caught by surprise as Elsa and Jimmy bend over and stare at the bloated, gruesome face. I come closer and read the caption claiming the death mask was taken off Villa as he lay dead in the Hidalgo Hotel in Parral. More people gather around me and we gaze at the closed eyes, the bloated cheeks, and the round face. The mask has been painted a bright, sick pink.

"Gather around, gather around," Martha orders as everyone listens. "This is the death mask of Francisco 'Pancho' Villa, one of the biggest villains these parts have ever known. Take a look at that face. The Columbus Historical Society is proud to say we have one of only five death masks made when he was gunned down by his own men."

His own men? Martha is excited and waves her clipboard in the musty air. "We don't know what happened to the other four death masks, but we are proud to own one of them. As for the other invaders, over here is an old newspaper article about the Mexicans that got hung up in Deming. Be sure to read it before you go. There are photos showing their fate. Yeah, they burned most of the bodies right down the street here, but they caught some of them and hung them in Deming. I think they hung about eighty Mexicans."

I laugh for the first time on the tour and Kay glares at me. Historical, government, and court records show only six Mexicans were hung. Some of my fellow tourists love these details Martha is giving us and are delighted, whispering and giggling among themselves. Elsa puts her straw hat back on her head before squeezing her way through the crowd and out the door. I wander through the three other rooms as people take bathroom breaks, while others buy souvenir cards and Columbus pencils, or sit on the benches outside the station. Kay and Martha are in constant quiet talk behind the counter when I go back to the room with the death mask. Kay's eyes follow me, even though her mouth doesn't miss a beat of fast conversation with Martha.

I am alone in front of the death mask. The heavy Mexican features are exaggerated by death, but Villa slightly resembles my grandfather Bonifacio. I'm sure of it. My mother has shown me enough family photos for me to know his high forehead, thick eyebrows, and wide nose. Is this plaster ghost what I have been searching for? Are the eccentric museum and fracturing of historical fact the legacy of the General on the border? Here is the final expression of Villa, whom so many people have chased over the century, casting him as deranged killer or hero and Robin Hood to the cause of Mexican freedom, their many views also turning him into ruthless politician, greedy bandit, and racist stereotype. The legend persists, is changed and twisted to fit what the Columbus Historical Society needs, and yet this eerily fascinating mold of a famous man is a swollen fossil from everything the border takes, destroys, and leaves behind in order to reinforce boundaries drawn in the sand by the clashing worlds of the United States and Mexico. The cameras and sensors may catch the next Pancho Villa sneaking across to start trouble or work for a few U.S. dollars, but the electronic sentries will never capture or document the dark and magnificent spirit that may be trapped in the death masks of every face that has fallen in the waterless deserts, the torn barrios, or the crime scenes of racial conflict. The repelling and magnetic moon face under glass keeps escaping through dry arroyos and blind spots in the Border Patrol grid. The more the death expression escapes across the desert, the more difficult it is to understand conflict on the border, or guess why this little train station in the middle of nowhere contains thousands of lifeless objects from the stories of U.S. and Mexican citizens who played out a tragic event. These tiny rooms of mounted and trapped history also show how Columbus's citizens and other westerners turn tragedy into a grand adventure that assures their livelihoods in the modern world. This dead man came from the lower classes of society, had little education, and organized no political party. Villa remains the only foreigner who has attacked the mainland of the United States since the War of 1812 and gotten away with it. His Division del Norte is still the largest revolutionary army that Latin America ever produced, at its peak numbering more than 150,000 soldiers, larger than any force Emiliano Zapata and Madero ever fielded during the revolution. The General's closed eyes and final letting go calmly collect dust in Columbus and are so far removed from great armies and larger-than-life stereotypes that rose out of that conflict.

My grandfather Bonifacio was fourteen years old in 1914 and living in Juárez when Villa's army took the border town in battle. They forced him and hundreds of other young men to join his army for the march south to continue the Chihuahua campaign. Bonifacio was rounded up at gunpoint and sheltered in a cattle pen with other conscripts. He escaped that night by leaping over the fence when Villa's guards fell asleep. Bonifacio crept through the dark streets of Juárez until he found the house of a friend and hid in his cellar for three days. Villa's army pulled out of the area without him and Bonifacio began his long journey across the Southwest. He wound up in Yuma, Arizona, where he worked in the Yaqui mines, the 118-degree heat of the Sonoran desert keeping him there until he went to work for the Union Pacific railroad in the early twenties.

When I exit the museum, Vinnie and Sarah are standing in the middle of the dirt street and pointing to the old army barracks west of the station. Camp Furlong, Army Post 1916, is now a set of crumbling buildings, low walls, and broken fences, abandoned by the U.S. military in 1926, though it was the place where the army's first biplanes flew during training for World War I. Why the military would choose Columbus as the place to try out a new airplane is beyond me. Perhaps the radar balloon floating in the sky is a sign they made the right choice.

Everybody hops back on the bus for the tour of Pancho Villa State Park. The area where the army base used to be has been turned into one of the most beautiful cactus gardens I have ever seen. It is almost noon and getting very hot. Al quickly turns on the air conditioning as his passengers sweat and fan themselves with their hats. The bus follows the dirt road past the train station and turns south toward the park's picnic grounds.

Kay is at it again. "Okay, everybody, I know it's hot, but we will be eating in Paloma soon. Isn't that museum amazing? Let's give Martha a big hand for talking to us."

Martha is back in the station, but we obediently clap as we leave her behind. Kay continues, "Camp Furlong housed the brave men who fought Villa and won the battle here. It was abandoned after World War I when most military operations were coming out of Fort Bliss in El Paso. You can see some of the buildings are still standing. The state of New Mexico and the local citizens of Columbus have done a wonderful job of turning this place into a beautiful park. The state dedicated the park in 1961." What Kay doesn't mention is local opposition to the name of the park when it opened, or the fact that then-state-senator Albert Amador of Española vowed to try to change the park's name because he considered Villa "an assassin without scruples who would destroy entire families without rhyme or reason."

The latest controversy in Columbus's struggle to become a hotbed of tourism took place in February of last year. An ambitious group of citizens decided to trace Villa's ride north to Columbus, trying to add to the three-decade tradition of residents marking the anniversary of the raid with the playing of taps and the recitation of the names of Americans killed in the battle. The reenactment was led by Allen Rosenberg, a member of the 13th Memorial Horse Cavalry, Inc., a nonprofit group in Columbus formed in 1998. Rosenberg stated to the *El Paso Times*, "We want to stimulate tourism so people in the area can make some money, including ourselves. The ride this year could be a healing process." They managed to get more than one hundred Mexicans, calling themselves the Villista Cavalcade, to ride on horseback from San Geronimo Hacienda, Mexico, the origin of Villa's route to Columbus. Leaving February 27 on a nine-day trek north, the cavalcade was joined by Chihuahua governor Patricio Martinez García for a flag exchange between U.S. and Mexican participants at Pancho Villa State Park. Members of the General John J. Pershing American Legion Post No. 1916 refused to participate in the flag exchange, so volunteers had to be found at the last minute.

The event was opposed by the Columbus Historical Society, who refused to participate and warned Rosenberg and his group not to have the riders appear in town between March 11 and 14, the days the society holds its annual commemorative events. City Council member Ramon Garcia Jr. told the *Times* he hated the idea because "Villistas come in and kill a bunch of our people and now we're making them heroes." It was supported by Columbus mayor Ken Riley, who joined Rosenberg in the *Times* by repeating, "We are working with Mexico trying to create a more friendly relationship. We want to promote tourism and industry in the area." Norma Gomez, director of the Columbus Chamber of Commerce, told the paper she viewed the ride from Mexico as an "economic development initiative." Rosenberg and his group hope to build a replica of Camp Furlong on a twenty-acre piece of Columbus land and re-create the lifestyle of Pershing's troops. The idea, Rosenberg explained, is "to attract tourists who are interested in spending a week living like a soldier of 1916."

I read this whole story in the *El Paso Times* a year and a half after it took place and shook my head, knowing that other cities have reacted in similar ways. When the Mexican government sent Tucson, Arizona, a fourteen-foot statue of Villa in 1981, the gift angered some New Mexicans and Arizonans who considered Villa nothing more than a celebrated bandit. Four years ago, tourism industry leaders in El Paso turned down a plan to adorn historic sites around town with statues of famous figures of the Wild West because one of the largest would have been a statue of the General on a horse.

Now, as I take in the tranquility of the unusual desert park, the divisions among the citizens of this desolate place come back. One week out here living like a soldier, sleeping under those thorns, with rattlesnakes and scorpions visiting your sleeping bag in the night, would certainly be a true western adventure. Play out your historical events, reenact them, and watch those divisions grow wider. We drive through the empty acres and I hear comments on the bus about "nothing out there but cactus thorns, sand, and heat." Someone else remarks he heard Martha say the Border Patrol recently buried more sensors too close to the park and they would disrupt business. There is no one out among the mass of cactus, so perhaps the added electricity has already done its job. My fellow travelers don't seem impressed with the magnificent growth of barrel, lechuga, ocotillo, and prickly pear cactus that spread throughout the park. Old wooden benches and picnic tables sit empty under several cottonwoods. Rosenberg's "healing process," eighty-five years after the raid, would probably require that the Historical Society clean out its museum and get rid of all the racist photos and mis-information lining its walls. To heal would mean destroying those photos of the Mexicans hung in Deming and the cartoon caricatures of Mexican bandits pasted on billboards, T-shirts, posters, and coffee cups all over El Paso and the Southwest. It could mean returning Villa's death mask to Mexico. Over Martha Billings's dead body!

Al takes the bus in a slow circle around the park and I am delighted with the beautiful, twisted mounds of cactus. Outside of the Saguaro National Park near Tucson, Arizona, I have never seen so many kinds of cactus clus-tered together. Stacks and knots of twisted plants rise ten to fifteen feet out of the flat, dry ground to decorate the park with enormous formations. I enjoy seeing them and think about money as sticky as prickly pears. The mayor, Rosenberg, and Gomez mentioned tourism and economic initiatives for the local citizens. Kay gets the ticket money for her business in El Paso and buses groups like ours out here. We get Martha and her museum, a circle around the cactus wonders, then a great meal in Palomas.

That is exactly what the Pink Restaurant gives us at noon. Al parks the bus in a dirt lot by the U.S. Customs checkpoint and we cross into Mexico on foot as two bored Mexican federales watch us enter their country. They don't bother to search the handbags some group members carry and act like they are used to seeing Kay herd bands of tourists across. I walk behind Elsa and Jimmy, the elderly man slowing down as the heat intensifies. The fourteen of us are used to the squalor and surreal imagery of border towns; comments about life in Juárez and El Paso drift throughout the bus during the trip. Palomas appears to be the size of four or five Juárez city blocks, though it extends beyond the shimmering waves of dust and heat, its dirty streets covered in trash and populated with street vendors, beggars asking for handouts, and silent Mexican men who lean against crumbling walls and stare at the march of the tourists.

No one explains why a restaurant in a Mexican town has an English name. It is located only two blocks from the entry point. The Pink Restaurant is one of the best Mexican diners I have eaten in, offering authentic cooking and cold beer. The group sits around a long table and the waiters bring ice water, chips, and salsa. Elsa and Jimmy talk at the end of the table and I sit next to Joe and Bernice Taylor, a quiet, middle-aged husband and wife from El Paso. During the meal, they tell me about their travels to California, other parts of Mexico, and a memorable drive to the mission church of Chimayo in northern New Mexico, where they brought back a sample of the holy dirt visitors can extract from the hole in the sanctuary floor. Legend has it the hole never runs out of dirt and the grains contain healing powers. The ancient adobe walls of the shrine are covered in thousands of milagros, medallions left there by grateful worshippers whose ailments and problems were cured with the holy dirt. Bernice bites into her enchilada and mumbles something about Joe not seeing the ghost of his grandfather Ramiro since they rubbed some Chimayo dirt on his forehead. I don't say anything and bite into my chile rellenos. People laugh, drink, and wander into the tourist shop at the front of the restaurant. Kay circles the table and shakes hands with each of us, thanking us for taking her tour, and wanting to know what we think.

"Great day, Kay!" Jimmy mutters. I notice he has downed his third shot of tequila. Elsa, Vinnie, and Sarah have each lined up two empty margarita glasses by their plates. Nobody asks Kay about Villa or Columbus, and I get the impression that for most of these people the goal of the trip is to find a good place to eat Mexican food besides the ones they regularly hit in Juárez. The four or five people who talk between bites inquire about Juárez nightclubs, the tour of El Paso haunted houses, and Kaye's plans for a Mesilla route. My chile rellenos are hot and delicious, and the meal is served with plenty of fresh tortillas. Kay announces we will spend twenty minutes here after everyone is done, then we must head back to Columbus and El Paso. I finish eating and wander around the shop. Like every border market, the restaurant sells jewelry, belts, piñatas, serapes, sombreros, statues of saints, and other crafts. Cheap tourist mementos are a thriving industry on the border and the prices in Palomas are cheaper than in Juárez.

I examine a pair of earrings I might buy for my wife and notice Jimmy stumbling out of the restaurant, heading by himself down the street. I don't pay further attention because I spot something high on one of the shelves in the far corner of the shop. The place is crowded with American tourists who have somehow made it to Palomas on their own, instead of joining the millions in Juárez, sixty miles to the east. I pass a young couple and their two children as the parents push the kids away to another part of the store. My curiosity about the rush at the back shelf increases.

On the highest shelf, set back from easy retrieval, are dozens of miniature clay statues of Aztec Indians having sex. Each figure is about four or five inches big, hand carved and painted, in every possible sexual position known to humans. Men and women Aztecs are joined in couples and threesomes, doing it doggy style, from above, sideways, and below. The artist has exaggerated the size of the men's genitals and the women's expressions of ecstasy. Women get it every which way and then some. Aztec warriors are serviced on knees, on all fours, and standing up. The sculptor knew what he or she was creating, though price stickers of only $2.50 are stuck on each figure. I have never seen anything like this set of Aztec sexual athletes and immediately think of Martha's museum. These fucking brown people would be ideal in glass cabinets across the border. Their orgasms could be part of a healing process in which everyone with an economic interest in the border takes the story back to the basic carnal instincts of people fucking each other. Preserve their desire in clay and glass and, of course, plaster death faces. Sex, death, and the reenactment of history. It fits what I have seen in Columbus and it is right here for only $2.50 per fuck.

I want to buy the whole set of fornicating Aztecs. I ponder this possibility until a sudden cry from Kay breaks my daydream. A drunk Jimmy stumbles into the restaurant with blood dripping down his left arm and a waiter tries to keep him on his feet.

"What happened?" Kay screams as several tour members gather around.

"Too much tequila!" Jimmy laughs and clutches his arm. "Boy, that's good stuff!"

Elsa breaks in and hugs the old man. "He told me he got medical shot in veterans hospital," she tells Kay in broken English. "His shot bleeding."

No one noticed Jimmy wearing a Band-Aid on his arm. He must have yanked it off in his drunk antics outside and opened the hole. Elsa sits him down and cleans the arm with a wet napkin and water.

"That's it, people," Kay commands. "Back to Columbus. Let's start walking back across the checkpoint. Remember you have to declare anything you buy."

The only purchases are bottles of tequila. With one arm around Jimmy, Elsa grabs her tequila bottle and guides Jimmy toward the door. Vinnie and Sarah carry two tequila bottles each. We exit into the piercing heat. I leave the fucking Aztecs behind and walk with Molly, the granddaughter of the Buffalo Soldier. She has been very quiet throughout the trip and I ask her what she thinks as we dodge an old pickup truck full of Mexican men. It churns past us in a cloud of dust, so we hurry across the street.

Molly smiles under her baseball cap. "Kay's got quite an operation here. I think the Mexican food was the best part. I've never been out here and had no idea Palomas and Columbus were so small."

I nod as several tour members stand in line to be checked through Customs. We enter an air-conditioned building where metal detectors and inspection stations welcome people crossing from Palomas.

"What did you think of the Pancho Villa Museum?" I ask Molly as we wait, the people who bought liquor slowing everybody down.

"I can't believe it," Molly says. "My grandfather never told me much about this area when I was a little girl. I think he spent most of his time in El Paso. Look at the kind of photos they got in there." Her voice rises. "Do you think a black Buffalo Soldier's picture or the things they went through in the army are going to hang in there?" She lowers her voice.

Elsa and Vinnie are carrying Jimmy by each shoulder, asking the stern U.S. Customs officer to forgive them for bringing a drunk through. Everyone passes and we board the bus for the ride back. Kay wipes sweat off her face and looks impatient as Al starts the engine. She grabs the mike, "We always do a quick little drive through some of Columbus's streets, then Martha will give us a final salute before we head back. Did everybody have a great meal?"

People nod and clap. Jimmy is asleep in a seat by himself, his head propped against the window, his cap low over his eyes. Vinnie and Sarah have taken a row farther back and have opened a bottle of tequila. I look again and can't believe how quickly the seal and tight cap have come off. Sarah sneaks a sip from the bottle and passes it to Vinnie. Elsa, sitting a couple of rows up from them, happens to turn and sees what they are doing.

She laughs, but Kay hasn't caught on. The rest of the passengers look sleepy and tired after the meal and the hot walk across. Most of them are nodding off, though Molly and the Taylors take everything in and are always alert. Sarah takes another shot and passes the bottle to Elsa, who grabs it without Kay noticing.

Al drives into the heart of Columbus, with its four or five small buildings per block, the streets unpaved except for the highway leading north to Deming and the one we took. "I know it looks deserted," Kay reads my mind, "but the hard-working citizens of Columbus are in Deming this time of day. You should see it on weekends. Lots of activity and things to do." Her mike whines and she holds it on her lap as Al stops in front of the Tumbleweed Theatre, its ancient walls painted a dull blue. The meeting hall of the famous American Legion Post 1916 is right next door.

"We always stop here to say hello to Bill Masefield, owner of the Tumbleweed. He is one of Columbus's finest businessmen and supporters of its history," Kay explains and opens the bus doors.

As if on cue, a bald, thin man who must be in his sixties rushes out of the theater and hops on board.

"Hi, darling!" Bill exclaims and gives Kay a bear hug. Elsa sips on the tequila and hands it back to Vinnie and Sarah. The two elderly women keep surprising me as they boldly drink from the bottle.

Bill waves to the passengers, who try to wake up. "Hello, everybody. I'm glad you've made it to Columbus, site of the famous Pancho Villa raid of 1916. Boy, we sure showed the General it doesn't pay to attack Columbus. I'm sure you've learned a great deal about the battle and had a chance to look at what we have to offer. Before you head back to good ole' El Paso, I just want to say thank you for coming and to remind you that we need people like Kay, her company, and folks like you to make sure our town keeps growing and keeps showing people how proud we are of our history. By the way, Columbus, New Mexico, can be proud to say we do not have one single sign of graffiti on our houses and buildings. That's right. No graffiti allowed in Columbus. Have a good ride back."

Bill pinches Kay's tight shorts and jumps off the bus. She waves goodbye and Al spins out of the lot toward the train station. No graffiti in Columbus? I had not even thought about it because the decrepit buildings and the mighty DEA drug balloon high in the air made me focus elsewhere. Martha is waiting for us outside the station with an impatient look. She wipes sweat off her face and climbs slowly into the bus.

"I want to thank you for coming to our town. Bill at the Tumbleweed and I appreciate your visit. Please tell people about our museum. It's a great place and like Bill told you, there is no graffiti. Good-bye!" She waves, pats Kay on the back, and leaves.

She knew what Bill told us. The coordinated, departing message about graffiti is delivered because we are heading back to the evil border town with its kingdom of crime and gangs. The air-conditioned air coming out of the ceiling hits me in the face. I take off my baseball cap and say good-bye to Columbus, which disappears in no time as Al races east on the highway. I take a last close look at the enormous balloon as Vinnie breaks out in a loud cackling. Sarah and Elsa join her and they laugh their way out of Columbus, the three of them drunk on the bottle that is already half empty!

Kay rises from her seat, takes a good look at the trio, and spots the bottle. Thinking she is going to explode, I put my cap back on. Kay holds on to the back of the seats and moves toward the drunk women. Vinnie slips her handbag over the bottle, trying to hide it in her lap. Kay stands next to her and breaks into a big smile.

"You think this is a first on this long ride?" Kay asks Vinnie and Sarah.

Both women's long white hair has tumbled out of their buns and over their happy, wrinkled faces. They laugh and spit, Sarah spasming into a guffaw she tries to smother. Vinnie cackles loudly again.

"Give me a taste," Kay demands and takes the bottle from Vinnie.

She sips it, makes a face and hands it back. She goes to the front of the bus and settles in for the ride. This must have done the trick because Vinnie puts the cap on the bottle and slips it inside her bag. No more drinking, though the two of them and Elsa laugh all the way to El Paso, waking the other passengers off and on.

The furnace of the desert is in full throttle as we trace border fences back to El Paso. I look beyond the barriers and the camera poles and try to imagine Villa's forces out there. The low hills and broken cliffs of distant mountains look more ominous on the Mexican side. I finally take a look at Kay's earlier handout. It is a three-page summary of Doroteo Arango's life and how he became the legendary Pancho Villa, written by Mitchell Friedlander, an El Paso writer. It is followed by a clear summary of the Mexican Revolution and Villa's role in it, though it doesn't mention the Columbus raid. The first page has a photo of Villa on horseback and the headline "Pancho Villa, the Mexican Robin Hood." The subtitle reads "In Villa's regiment, there were several American mercenaries with such names as Tray Richardson, Oscar Creighton, and Sam Dregen—all hell-raising gringos who rode with Villa for both gold and adventure."

The hour-and-a-half drive to El Paso is uneventful except for the three drunks who look out the window and laugh at landscapes flying by. Kay is too tired to say much over the mike and Al doesn't get lost. We pull into the Convention Center around three in the afternoon. Jimmy is helped off the bus and disappears into the men's bathroom. Vinnie and Sarah are picked up by Sarah's daughter, who has a shocked expression on her face as she helps the two women into her car. Elsa walks alone toward San Jacinto Plaza, and other passengers go their own ways across the burning pavements of downtown. Kay rushes into the trolley office without saying good-bye and I am disappointed at how fast everybody has disappeared.

"You never told me what you do or why you came on this fun ride," Molly asks me as she climbs off the bus. I have been standing there, hesitant to go find my car in the underground parking lot.

"I'm originally from El Paso, lived here most of my life, but I had never been to Columbus," I tell her. "I teach at the University of Minnesota."

"Minnesota? That's so far way," Molly says and pulls car keys from her purse. "What did you learn going to Columbus for the first time?"

I'm not sure what to answer as we head for the garage. "I learned that Pancho Villa is dead and well in Columbus."

Molly, granddaughter of a Buffalo Soldier, laughs. "I know exactly what you mean." She waves good-bye and finds her car.

Would Bar Pictures of General Villa's Body from City Windows
A movement should be started to remove from El Paso store windows the gruesome pictures of Pancho Villa and his companions who were killed at Parral, Ponder S. Carter, corporation court attorney, declared.

—*El Paso Herald*, July 31, 1923

10,339 El Pasoans View Villa Movie

Up to six P.M. yesterday, 10,339 persons had seen "Viva Villa," the picturization of the life of Pancho Villa, famed Mexican rebel leader, at the Ellanay Theater. The picture has attracted larger audiences than any shown in El Paso in recent years.

—*El Paso Times,* May 3, 1934

Rough Rider Denies Villa in Regiment

Pancho Villa, Mexican rebel chieftain, never served in Roosevelt's Rough Riders, declares radio patrolman Alvin C. Ash, member of the famous band of soldiers. He thinks Robert L. Ripley, in his "Believe It or Not" column is mistaken.

—*El Paso Herald Post,* May 17, 1934

Mass for Villa

Mass was said today in the Church of Our Lady of Guadalupe in Juárez for Francisco Villa, one-time guerilla chieftain and Mexican revolutionary leader. Today is the 17th anniversary of Villa's assassination in Parral, Chihuahua. Arrangements for the mass were made by two of Villa's former soldiers, Pedro Roberto Lopez and Aguiles Pereyra.

—*El Paso Herald Post,* January 20, 1941

It is one year later and it has taken that long to get to the History Museum at the east end of the city. I have returned to El Paso three times since the Columbus tour, busily exploring my hometown, the desert, and writing about it. Each time I come back, various Villa references remind me I am not done. The latest was a question on the game show "Jeopardy." I was getting dressed in the guest room of my mother's house. The television was on and I happened to hear the answer, "He was the last foreign invader to attack the United States." The category is twentieth-century American history. The contestant answers, "Who was Pancho Villa?" The General on Jeopardy! That's it—the final push.

As I said, the proclaimed death mask in the El Paso museum is not the same face as the one in Columbus. I search the empty place with its long corridors and rows of displays, but there is no one around. After circling the entire museum, I finally spot an elderly woman in a back office near the gift shop counter. She comes out and asks if I am buying anything. I shake my head, having checked out the lousy selection of books on local history.

"Do you know about the Pancho Villa death mask in there?" I point to the Mexican Revolution exhibit.

She grimaces. "Pancho Villa? The bandit?"

I nod. "Do you know how they got the death mask? Has anyone ever checked with the Columbus museum about their mask?"

The woman does not like this. "Death mask? Columbus museum? We don't have anything on Christopher Columbus."

"Thank you," and I leave.

Later that afternoon, I sit at a quiet table in the rare books archives of the UTEP library. Donald Chavez, the librarian, gets excited when I mention Villa and tells me the university holds dozens of photographs about him, the revolution, and his assassination. He brings out three archival boxes and I spend a couple of hours going through them. I have seen many of them reproduced in history books—black-and-white photos of revolutionaries, cutthroat politicians, and dead soldiers in dusty streets. I ask Chavez about Columbus, but he says they don't have any photos on the raid, except for pictures of General Pershing and his men at Fort Bliss.

"Has UTEP ever collected stuff on the Columbus raid or information on the death mask they have in their museum?"

He sorts through more old photos. "I've been here ten years and have never seen anything, though years ago some professor told me a bunch of photos and documents on Columbus disappeared from the collections when the library was in the old building and we didn't have the kind of security we have now. He said this was back around 1975 or 1976."

He leaves to help other visitors and I find a set of photos on Villa's death. The first one shows his car riddled with bullet holes. The next is similar to the ones in Columbus, with empty streets and people gathered around. The third one is a find. Villa's body hangs upside down out of the shattered car, his bullet-torn body facing the camera, both arms extended toward the ground, his legs hooked inside the vehicle to hold him there. I look closer and grab the magnifying lens that comes with the archival boxes and study the photo again. It is a very old and faded picture with shadows from shocked townspeople covering parts of Villa's profile. Seven or eight onlookers surround the car. I can't tell, but it looks like his face caught several bullets. Chavez has disappeared in the stacks. I blink and strain my eyes through the magnifying glass. I can't decide. Did some of the sixteen bullets Villa was reported to have taken shatter his face? The death masks in Columbus and El Paso are of a man, or two men, with smooth features bloated in death, but not broken by bullet holes. If a death mask is molded as soon as possible after death, there would not be time for a doctor or conspirator to cover the wounds.

I sit for another fifteen minutes with the photo of Villa, the General resembling a dead deer a hunter propped over the car hood for a trophy portrait. Chavez appears and I return the photos to their files. I mention the awful image of Villa hanging out of the car and Chavez says it was one of four brutal photos that became a set of best-selling postcards not long after Villa's assassination. He adds that the original cards are collectors' items and recalls old-timers talking about the notorious murder scenes selling like hotcakes in El Paso in the mid-twenties because people wanted proof the evil man was really dead. I thank him when he asks if I found what I needed and leave.

It is almost four P.M. and rush-hour traffic has slowed to a crawl, but I return to the History Museum before it closes. I put another two-dollar donation in the box and hurry to the glass cabinet. The old woman is gone, replaced by a high-school-age boy behind the counter. I find the cabinet and get down on my knees for a better view. The first time I had to rely on the photograph next to the death mask, because the mask was face down. On the second visit, I jump to my feet, because someone has turned the mask face up. Did the woman I questioned fix it? Perhaps another visitor reported that the mask couldn't be seen upside down. The General looks at me with closed eyes. Pancho Villa in Columbus. Pancho Villa in El Paso. Two different towns connected by the same border. Two different museums with their own death masks. Chavez would not let me photocopy any of the archival photos, but I don't need to look at the grisly assassination scene again to decide the General is alive and well on the border.

Part Three

The Death of the Poet

I listen to the Doors' cryptic saga, "The End." It is a dark, ten-minute song made famous as part of the sound track to Francis Ford Coppola's Vietnam nightmare film, *Apocalypse Now*. Jim Morrison screams "All the children are insane waiting for the sacred rain!" I have not played the song in years. I am searching for hidden meaning in a 1966 rock-and-roll song by a band whose music sells better today than it did when Morrison was alive. "Ride the snake," he hisses. The poet is dead. He has been dead for thirty years. All of a sudden, he is stalking his mother down the hall. Then, the famous lyrics seethe out of his sweating throat, "Father, I want to kill you. Mother, I want to fuck you!" Explosions. Music. Chaos. The dying slash of Morrison's spirit. The poet is dead, dying at the end of the century as his music plays on.

In my hometown of El Paso, two sixteen-year-old boys died from jimson weed poisoning last June. The hallucinogenic and dangerous plant is a popular drug among kids today. They call it "crazy weed" or "loco weed." The boys boiled a bagful of weed roots and drank a cup each, then wandered off by themselves and were found dead the next morning. Friends of theirs who drank small amounts said they experienced hallucinations, including one in which imaginary people appeared to them. Jimson weed is legal and free and is a roadside weed that grows all over the desert. Officials in Washington, D.C., reported 318 jimson weed poisoning cases last year. The desert is getting its revenge in a manner Jim Morrison could appreciate because the poets are dying but have found a way to do it by being in touch with "nature." Forget the native rituals of peyote and the hippies who took it in the sixties and seventies. This is a different trip. The streets and houses of El Paso keep spreading and cutting into the landscape—a stark terrain whose beauty and solitude is offered to poets who want to die in the desert. Who knows what those boys saw when they went over the limit. It must have been quite a blazing entrance, where the dead from the ancient past wait for them to get off the desert floor, dust the sand off their clothes, and keep flying toward another desert where jimson weed is never needed.

My grandmother Julia died in El Paso at the age of ninety-six on May 8, 2000, the same day as the Mexican observation of Mother's Day. The night before she died, I had a disturbing dream that made me cry out in my sleep until my wife shook me awake. In that other world, there was the shadow or shape of someone trying to climb into the bedroom window toward me. Was it Julia coming to say good-bye hours before she left?

The viewing at the funeral home was full of silence, except for my grand-aunt Consuelo, Julia's sister, who was helped to the open casket by cousins of mine who had not visited my grandmother in more than thirty years. Consuelo wailed, "You left me alone! You left me alone!" No one answered in the midst of tears and numerous gift baskets of flowers, this outcry the conclusion to a rocky relationship between the two sisters. They didn't want to live in the same barrio apartment together after thirty years, so eight years ago my mother took my grandmother in. "They drove us away! They drove us away!" Consuelo wails in reference to her falling out with my mother over funeral arrangements and years of her and my Uncle Benito's cruel treatment. My mother's sister and brothers refused to help pay the thousands of dollars in funeral costs, so the money came from my mother, my sisters, and me. I sat in one of the back pews and thought about family dynamics as I studied members of my family I had not seen since childhood, concluding I would never find out what split everybody apart decades ago.

A few years ago, in a letter to the *New York Times Book Review,* the poet Samuel Hazo blasted a reviewer for praising a new book by John Ashbery, one of America's most worshipped poets. Hazo snapped at the reviewer for proclaiming Ashbery a visionary who writes poems "that come close to God's own work." Hazo listed ten poets he felt were better. He said he was tired of people praising a writer whose work was an exercise in what he called "fancy boredom." It is the kind of letter that will get a huge reaction from Ashbery loyalists. According to some critics and poets, the poet is dying. On the other hand, his followers say he is alive and well. It is the same old story: Which poet is genuine? Who can set the reviewer straight about all this? Someone has to pay for the fact that the poet is dying.

Yet the poet rises in unexpected places. In the same issue of the *Times,* there was a feature article on corporate America producing a growing number of serious poets. The reporter said the wide range of poets in the business field is coming from the tradition of T. S. Eliot, a banker, and Wallace Stevens, who sold insurance. Several poets like John Barr, an investment banker, and insurance executive Ted Kooser are interviewed. Donald Everett Axinn, a real estate developer, talks about his experiences in the business and poetry world. Barr claims he rises at three every morning to work on poems before the phone starts ringing. Kooser, with a long career in the literary world, says he shares drafts of poems with his fellow workers and secretaries in the office. If someone questions the clarity of a line or metaphor, he rewrites the poem. He brings poetry to the insurance world. He has an audience. Axinn, whose poetry has not received the respect of Kooser's, says, "The poem and the office building both require structural form." Which comes first, the office or the poem?

Another poet who is interviewed is Dana Gioia. His poetry is very conservative, formal, and academic. He is a former vice-president of Kraft General

Foods. Gioia is also a translator and a literary critic. He is the author of a highly acclaimed book of essays on poetry, *Does Poetry Matter?* The book includes two memorable essays. One deals with the fact that the poetry audience in this country is very small. He wonders if anyone is buying books of poetry. What Gioia seems to resent most is that poets have made poetry into a business—fellowships, grants, awards, hundreds of new books of poems every year. Gioia is a businessman. His other memorable essay is a call for the literary world not to forget Weldon Kees. His empty car was found near the Golden Gate Bridge in 1959. No one has seen Kees since. His haunting poems can be found in an obscure *Collected Poems*. The poet is dead, but Gioia wants him back.

In the *Times* article, Gioia says, "Despite what people in the arts think, the contemporary business world is full of first-rate artistic talent. They have made careers in business because of the career uncertainties of the arts world." When it comes to careers and making a living, Gioia's statement is correct. Except for Kooser's long and outstanding body of work, none of these businessmen who were interviewed are strong poets. The poem by Barr included in the piece is embarrassing. He is going to be the first business-man to head the Poetry Society of America, the country's oldest poetry association, with 2,500 members. It may be the perfect position for a corpo-rate type. Though the organization sponsors several national poetry compe-titions, it does have a reputation for catering to amateur poets and dreadful "dilettantes." The reporter listed Barr's publications, but did not include the fact that the presses that published his books are vanity presses. The poet is dying and his spirit is going up in a high-rise, corporate building. He has pressed the button for the fortieth or fiftieth floor. A brand-new laptop computer waits for him at his desk.

The priest wore white and gold and spoke in rapid Spanish I could not follow. The casket was draped in white and silver, and the altar glittered as if something was going to continue between the cracked, peeling statues. Something in the church wanted to come alive, though it was already dying, some of the voices already dead. San Martín de Porres fell off the wall, but the crash was buried by the Spanish condemnation of anything that moves in the soul without permission. The poet must be shifting positions in the cosmos and is waiting for the turn of the century when poetry from the desert is transformed into passages where family history and Rio Grande myths no longer need to be written. He is now writing new poems on the computer screen and has abandoned the decades-old process of composing poetry by hand in his sacred notebooks. He is not a business type, yet he is writing faster poems that he composes spontaneously on the screen, words and lines and stanzas typed, printed, and erased faster than the jimson weed territories of troubled being. It must have something to do with wondering which doors the jimson weed opened for those stupid kids, or why Jim Morrison pulled a fast one on millions of fans when he was alive because he claimed he was a poet, too.

The priest raised his open arms as if he were Christ on the cross, pointing to the bleeding man several times in reference to the grandmother who was hiding under the Spanish vowels, her white hair the road I took entering the church, carrying her casket as if the weight of the pallbearer was the final gift from someone who had given me a great deal. The occasional sobbing flowed in a strange language I could not follow, except for the sound of the pallbearers heaving and raising the casket toward the hearse. These six men were blinded in the bursting leaves of sunlight that bounced off a thousand igniting shrouds, like fire from a throat that was sore from crying silently in a Spanish hush I last heard when I was one year old.

To get away from my family's intense preparations for my grandmother's funeral, I go for a drive into the desert north of El Paso. As I gaze toward distant landscapes, I listen to a story on NPR about Barbie dolls. The reporter is interviewing a man in the Midwest who owns two thousand Barbie dolls. He is only one of thousands of serious collectors. He says he likes the fashions that are available with Barbie dolls, but only uses his dolls as mannequins. Unlike other collectors interviewed on the program, he does not put emotional value on or name his dolls. The reporter, a woman, asks him if he dresses the dolls himself. "Of course," he answers, and says he even "undresses them sometimes." The reporter interrupts and says, "Let's not get into that right now."

She talks to organizers of national Barbie conventions and to the publisher of *Barbie Bazaar,* a serious fan magazine for adult collectors. She consults with two leading experts on the "underground" industry of the largest selling toy doll in the world. As I get stuck in rush-hour traffic, stunned by what I am hearing, the experts talk about some of the ups and downs in the thirty years of Barbie history. One of them mentions the time Mattel, the company that has made billions off the blonde bombshell, came out with black and Hispanic Barbies. They were introduced in 1980. Before that, it was caucasians only. The female expert praises Mattel for having hired a black woman to design the dark-skinned doll. Despite that, she says, the black Barbie's features still look very European. The best the designer could do was to include beads, short Afro hair, and bright clothes to promote the new line of "sister" Barbies.

My traffic light turns green and the expert says Mattel hit bottom with the Hispanic Barbie. She says they all looked like Carmen Miranda. Their chocolate skins are dim compared to the bright shawls, hats with bananas and other fruit, and the striped skirts. Two months ago, my wife and I went to the opening of a new K-Mart Superstore in town. When the poets are dying, they go to K-Mart. My wife noticed a Native American Barbie in the toy department. She actually wanted to buy it! The skin is not red, but brown. Just as on the black and Hispanic Barbies, the beautiful blue eyes stand out on this one. Even her long, braided hair can't detract from those beautiful blue eyes.

In the death song, the poet writes, "Don't think about generations of fertilization, the mother going back to the mother, fathers absent and busy with their own dying. The scent of the abyss is a disguised symbol for the one who has left us for good, dressed in a beautiful print dress with flower patterns, the image of the long white hair the one vision that won't go away, appearing and reappearing in shattered dreams floating above her open casket. Even the relatives who show up after forty years know who you are, and their orange tears have something to do with the way they ignored you for four decades. They have come for the grandmother body, too. Give them a shovel. There is plenty of soil to go around." Yet they don't get to ride in the funeral procession from the viewing to the church; the black limousine is reserved for my sisters, my mother, and me. The one-hundred-degree heat is blocked by dark windows in this powerful air-conditioned ride, with the quiet driver from the home. Don't cross your arms over your heart as the route takes the train of cars with headlights on through one of the worst barrios in south

El Paso—bombed-out tenement houses, graffitied freeway pillars, junked cars rusting in front yards surrounded by bright flowers, the area devastated by a border poverty everyone claims.

A few years ago, two friends of ours at the university where my wife and I were students had a baby boy. Pablo was their second son. His father was the only professor at the university who acknowledged me as a writer and used my books in his courses, and we became friends. My wife and I bought a gift for the new baby and had dinner at the couple's home a few weeks after the birth. We got to see the tiny baby and went home wishing we had children of our own. Two weeks later, Pablo died suddenly. The next day, my wife came home from teaching to give me the news. We went to the funeral two days later, then attended a reception at the same house where we had celebrated the birth one month before.

The poet is dying. The poet can't set foot anywhere because time is a blur and the earth is shifting with the grief of not understanding the order of things, how the desert delivers reality, then takes it away from the love of family and the love of history that has grown from the stories of families in the desert.

In his essay "Theory and Function of the Duende," the Spanish poet Federico García Lorca wrote, "These dark sounds are the mystery, the roots thrusting into the fertile loam known to all of us, ignored by all of us, but from which we get what is real in art." The dying poet does not know what is real in art, but he knows Jim Morrison represented something he could never have by simply writing poems. Jimi Hendrix had it and so did Janis Joplin; John Lennon and Jerry Garcia joined them not long after—poets of electric desire that has nothing to do with pulling the wrong vegetation from the sand and stuffing it down your throat, the electric canyons of yesterday teaching you to imitate song lyrics from stage lights that can never shine on what you are, even if you have stood in front of hundreds of people and recited your poetry.

The dying poet has a gift and a mystery, a sacred calling that rewards and punishes him when he is not listening to the Doors' music or imagining what it must have been like to see Hendrix and Joplin live on stage, poetic desire destroyed and replaced by rock-and-roll worship, a reaching for the stars the average poet will never obtain. Lorca says the duende "is not in the throat; the duende surges up from the soles of the feet." He insists the duende surges through your blood "like powdered glass" and tells us the duende does not come from angels or from muses. He declares we can be guided by angels and dictated to by the muse, but they don't have duende.

As a poet, I have written about death many times, but it has been the death of others until my grandmother's death. My death and the arrival of the dangerous word that trembles in the blood and destroys any false existence we live because of our past: things in the present give us the sense the world is crazy, and we wonder why all this is happening.

The NPR story on Barbie fades as I pull into the Fort Selden State Monument Museum. I wander through the ruins, then take several tourist brochures to add to the several hundred I have collected over the years. The "Summer 2000 New Mexico Vacation Guide" stands out from the stack. Pages 20 through 28 contain a chart of important events in New Mexico history. The time line borders the bottom of these pages from left to right with dates and photographs of the events. The tops of the pages are filled with advertising for resort hotels, travel agencies, points of interest, and information for tourism in New Mexico, a multibillion-dollar industry. I flip casually through it and stop on page 26. The six items highlighted include the most monumental event in state history, yet when the magazine lines up the detonation of the first atomic bomb alongside UFOs and a popular 1950s television show, the time line becomes an absurd capsule of occurrences and people that illustrate why New Mexico is the strange place that it is. Jim Morrison would fit right in.

The events on page 26 and 27 are, from left to right:

1939–1945: Navajo "code talkers" use their native language to confuse the Japanese army in World War II.

1945: Scientists detonate the world's first atomic bomb at Trinity Site near Alamogordo. Meanwhile, Georgia O'Keeffe buys a house in Abiquiu.

1947: A flying saucer reportedly crashes on a rancher's property near Corona and Roswell.

1950: Ralph Edwards challenges any city in the United States to rename itself after his game show "Truth or Consequences." Hot Springs,

New Mexico, rises to the occasion and changes its name to Truth or Consequences.

1958: Buddy Holly records some of his greatest hits in a studio in Clovis.

1986: Georgia O'Keeffe dies in Santa Fe at the age of ninety-eight.

That is it. If you have never been to New Mexico, the events highlighted on these pages should convince you to come to the Land of Enchantment. Navajos, atomic bombs, great artists, UFOs, TV game-show hosts, and legendary rock-and-roll pioneers make New Mexico a great place to visit. These highlights from the twentieth century, and the colorful way they are presented, are certain to overshadow jimson weed statistics. This could be the human touch every tourist guide should include, but what about the flying saucer? Plus, this is the first tourist magazine I have seen that uses a dominating photograph of a mushroom cloud to promote the wonders of the Southwest. There is ecotourism. How about nuke-tourism? Visit the Atomic Museum in Albuquerque, and replicas of Fat Man and Little Boy, the bombs dropped on Japan, will greet you. The poet is dying from radiation that will outlive his greatest poems, the language of eternity originating at ground zero, the same spot where he was born.

One of the last Navajo code talkers still alive in 2000 was interviewed recently, and he claims their language was used in codes only once against the Japanese. He said U.S. Army experts were too racist and territorial to use the Navajo language often. Georgia O'Keeffe was blind during the final years of her life and was taken care of by Juan Hamilton, a strange drifter who kept people from visiting O'Keeffe and inherited most of her artwork. Truth or Consequences is one of the weirdest and scariest towns I have ever visited in New Mexico. It is something straight out of the "X Files." There is a museum in town that contains a wax statue of Geronimo; the town was in the news in 1999 because of a man and woman who enslaved several women there and sexually assaulted them. Buddy Holly was from Texas. This leaves the UFOs. The year 1947 was a big one for flying saucers in New Mexico as dozens were sighted all over the state and at least three crashes were reported, though two of them never became as well known as the Roswell crash. Go visit the UFO Museum in Roswell to learn the whole story.

The state's tourist industry has accepted every aspect of its fabricated history. One section of the time line says, "Los Alamos National Laboratory and the ancient Bandolier Cliff Dwellings contrast each other in the wooded canyons of the Jemez Mountains." Nuclear weapons and the homes of a culture that mysteriously disappeared are singled out, side by side. The rest of the paragraph says, "While in Albuquerque, highly technological Sandia National Laboratories sits across the Rio Grande from the primitive rock art found at Petroglyph National Monument on the West Mesa."

Nuke-tourism is best represented by the last image I focus on before closing the magazine and driving back to El Paso to face the burial. It is the mushroom cloud. I study the whole graphic layout and stop at the top of the Trinity explosion. Whoever designed the page cropped the cloud at the top of the photo, where the blue background of another listing begins. The category called Birdwatching floats above the mushroom. It reads "Birdwatching—National Audubon Society," then gives the address, which ends as the atomic explosion takes over the glossy page.

Like the radiation of time and death, the transparent rosary melts in the heat on the way to the new cemetery, where recent graves rise twenty-five miles east of my mother's house, a place in the desert I never would have guessed as the final resting place of a woman who knew the desert for almost one hundred years. The dying poet continues his death song: "The melted rosary is going to teach you how to believe in the hip bone that survives centuries, going to make you recite new passages for the sphinx they found six feet under, its soiled smile a caricature of who is really going to lie there. Don't look when they pull the damn thing out of the ground to make room for the new burial. Parts of it will stay down there for several centuries, its arms, stone face, and fertile hips broken off and hiding underground to welcome the skeleton of profiles, the womb of yesterday, its closed fields sleeping in the earth to wait for the family to be born again. You will stay down there and lift the casket from the hearse, the priest asking each pallbearer to remove his white flower from his lapel and place it on the casket as the final act, my mother and sisters sitting on folding chairs closest to the hole in the ground they keep covered and won't show us, the digging that took place thousands of generations ago, the procedure of waiting for relatives to say their polite good-byes to one another and leave, so the clay bowl of birth can be lowered and released, plenty of soil lying around for family members who turn their backs and walk away. The white flower from your lapel will make you wake up in the night to watch the burning horse arrive, this sudden animal uninvited to the procession, forgotten as the one Julia rode across the border as an eight year old, its smoking prance of defiant muscle flattening the ground with clouds of fresh earth as if joy also deserved a perfumed casket."

Lorca is dead. Jim Morrison is dead, along with a million guitar heroes who cut the first landscapes of writing out of a desert childhood, until I wrote them back and turned up the volume on what they sang to me. In the end, did he have duende when he screamed for his mother? Am I even close to understanding what burning torches like Lorca and Morrison may have tried to tell me decades before my grandmother died? The poet is dying inside and the business of poetry and the business of abandoning the desert have cleared the path, scented the flowers, and declared new challenges. Lorca states, "The appearance of the duende always presupposes a radical change of all forms based on old structures. It gives a sensation of freshness wholly unknown, having the quality of a newly created rose, of miracle, and produces in the end an almost religious enthusiasm."

Faith is full and vibrant in the dying poet. He finally understands why boys want to drink jimson weed and be truly alive. He nods in approval when Americans collect plastic dolls. There is still time to believe the miracle of starting over is possible with poetry and with the passing of an old ghost whose long, white hair, now lying under the ground, has threaded hundreds of poems out of the poet for too long. Lorca also wrote, "A dead person in Spain is more alive when dead than is the case anywhere else—his profile cuts like the edge of a barber's razor." Later on he concludes, "The duende does not appear if it sees no possibility of death, if it does not know that it will haunt death's house, if it is not certain that it can move those branches we all carry, which neither enjoy nor ever will enjoy any solace." Solace for the dying poet tearing dry branches off the cottonwood near the site where the jimson boys died, but at least forty miles from the fresh funeral plot, its brown earth darker than the other graves around it—these meetings with the soil a transformation for someone who has given his soul to poetry without understanding, until now, that poetry comes after life because the poet has died to live.

Ten Crows

Ida and I are driving to Duluth for the weekend. She is at the wheel, so it gives me a chance to study the changing landscape from Minneapolis to Lake Superior, 150 miles away. The wooded slopes and long prairies north of the Twin Cities go by and the terrain starts to change, with more trees and fewer meadows as we get closer to Duluth. We speed along the highway and I notice the first crow on the right shoulder of the road. It is a large bird; from afar I think it is a dead animal. As we get closer, I see it is a crow walking along the shoulder in the odd, arrogant style of crows. It disappears into the tall grass as we rush by and I chuckle at its roadside manners.

About five miles later, a second crow is doing the same thing on the same side of the road. I wonder how often crows get hit hopping along the road, because road kills seem to be animals of every kind, except these birds. I don't point out the dumb crows to Ida because we are talking about something else. The miles rush by and I see a third and fourth crow within ten miles of each other, the two of them skipping and searching the shoulder of the highway. I start keeping track of the distance between these walkers and mention it to Ida, who says they are scavenging for remains of dead animals and wonders if I have better things to do than count crows all the way to Duluth. I sit up because it never occurred to me that even though the road kills may be gone, the crows are either hungry or desperate enough to peck at the tiniest traces of dead animals. The highway is clean and I have not seen any road kills, not even deer, as you often find on suburban streets in the Twin Cities. These crows must be desperate to peck at smeared remains because there are no fresh kills on the road. The four crows vanish into the yellow grass at the roadside and never take flight as our car swooshes by. I carefully count the number of crows walking along the road between Minneapolis and Duluth, something I admit is odd behavior, but recent travels through different parts of the country have awakened my interest in studying roadside patterns.

Over the next hundred miles, I watch for crows and tell Ida how various parts of the country differ in terms of dead animals on highways. If these crows in Minnesota were scraping the asphalt for last winter's remains, they would have a feast in southern New Mexico—land of road kills and territory for more dead dogs on roads than any other place I have been. I don't know if the desert is a dangerous region for strays wandering loose or whether parts of New Mexico are so isolated that road kills stay where they died for a longer period of time before they are cleaned up by the highway department. To identify highway driving in parts of southern New Mexico with dead dogs instead of beautiful mountain or desert vistas is an awful way to think of the area. It is one that fits the image of the West as rough and wild, where life is cheap. Yes, I am talking about dogs, not humans, though the West, with its constant clash of cultures, has certainly left more than its share of human casualties across the deserts of New Mexico, Arizona, and west Texas.

Traveling through fifty miles of La Mesilla Valley, between El Paso and

Las Cruces, I once passed over a dozen dead dogs whose carcasses lay in the middle of the road in various stages of decay. This is gruesome to write about, but the area and streets around the small town of Chamberino, in La Mesilla Valley, were dotted with dead dogs. They were almost as common as descansos, those crosses and flowery markers placed on highways by relatives of people who died in car crashes that dot the state. Fresh flowers, wooden crosses painted white, the names of the dead, and the dates of their violent deaths are a frequent sight in the Southwest. You can drive a busy freeway like Interstate 10 and count the descansos mounted in the grassy median between the north and southbound lanes, or weave through a two-lane back road along the Rio Grande, negotiating a blind curve between cotton and lettuce fields to pass a beautiful descanso on the shoulder of the deadly turn. On my last trip to Chamberino, I counted seven descansos, some several years old, between El Paso and the town—seven traffic fatalities reminding me that New Mexico roads are deadly as I also kept track of those twelve dead dogs, a few lying within a few yards of descansos.

Chamberino is a scary little town on a back road between Mesilla and Anthony, New Mexico. It was caught in the middle of historic events when the United States made the Gadsden Purchase in 1854. Chamberino was located in the middle of 77,000 square miles of Mexican land the United States bought for ten million dollars. The Gadsden Purchase created a new international boundary along the Rio Grande, and residents of Chamberino, having lived in old Mexico all their lives, found themselves living in New Mexico and the United States upon the signing of the purchase. Many residents of the town still do not speak English, and it retains an ancient, colonial atmosphere despite the hostility I sensed there. In addition to the farm and dairy products of rich Mesilla Valley, Chamberino boasts La Viña Winery, the oldest winery in New Mexico. Its grapes and wines are said to rival those grown in California.

During my high school years in El Paso, this back road of Highway 28 was my favorite drive out of the city. Thirty years later, there are new housing developments, golf courses, and a brand new freeway interchange going west from I-10 to Santa Teresa. Completed in the fall of 2000, the highway destroyed my beloved 28, blocking the route to Mesilla and Las Cruces forever. In contrast to the romantic appeal of the old road I had known for forty years, Chamberino is a black hole off the highway, hidden below a volcanic plateau west of the river.

On the way into town, I pass four dead dogs on the highway. Two of them look like recent kills and signal I have entered a no-man's-land of empty fields, dry irrigation canals, and looming black cliffs, their volcanic beds eroding into breeding grounds for rattlesnakes. The low, hard hills rise west of the town. Chamberino is built around an ancient, historic church I want to visit, but I have to pass through residential streets of crumbling adobe and wooden houses, each one guarded by barbed wire fences and heavy iron gates. Most of them have large, vicious dogs tied to ropes or chains in the front yards. Every other front yard is filled with two or three cars, most of them missing tires and mounted on cement blocks, their rusting or broken bodies in various stages of mechanical repair or outright abandonment. House after tiny house looks the same—the snarling dogs, impenetrable fences, and suspicious men, women, and children standing in their yards. They stop whatever they are doing to watch me drive down their streets. It is uncanny how each person freezes and pays careful attention to the stranger in the rental car who gawks back at them because he has never seen so many people stop what they are doing to look at him.

Their suspicion could come from a combination of poverty and paranoia; this area is a notorious crossroads for drugs coming north from Mexico. Combined with the distrust is curiosity, the two constantly at war with each other. Run-down Chevys and tough dogs protect groups of men in dirty T-shirts, who sit on porches drinking beer. When I turn a corner onto the next street, there is another dead dog lying against the curb. Graffiti decorates many of the houses, and glass from broken beer bottles shimmers up and down the streets. I don't want to think about what would happen if I got a flat tire in the middle of these neighborhoods.

Mad dogs start barking at me, until a chorus marks my slow drive toward the church. The wild sounds strain out of their vicious jaws, and two German shepherds snarl at each other in one driveway because they can't get to my car. Some of the animals are ready to break their chains. One enormous Doberman pinscher lunges against the metal fence of its owner's yard, leaps at least four feet off the ground, and bounces against the top of the fence, almost hooking its chain up there and hanging itself. A huge Mexican man screams at it from his doorway as I pass. The Doberman goes nuts when its owner yells, and it spins in a rapid circle, its chain caught in its long legs. Through my closed window, I can hear dog chains rattling and heavy bodies slamming to the ground when the big dogs pull too far. I turn onto another street and almost run over a huge, dead Doberman with legs twisted in the air, a powerful snarl frozen on its face. Before I reach the stone building of the peaceful church, in contrast to the hostility of the rest of the town, another dead dog, a small one, greets me near the church parking lot, its mangled fur blowing quietly in the hot breeze.

This last dog makes me want to speed away, but the quiet church calls to me. I circle its dirt lot, searching for a place to park near the entrance, in case I have to run inside quickly. I park, but change my mind about getting out when a massive, black rottweiler appears from behind the church and starts barking viciously at me, its large head distorted by the wide open jaws and the enormous white teeth. It is not tied to anything and stands guarding the church, each tremendous bark making it slide forward on the gravel. As I begin to turn the car around in the lot to head out of town, an old priest comes out of a side door and yells something to the dog. It stops barking and limps passively to its master, who pats its ugly head, then waves to me. I can't tell if he is signaling it is safe to enter the church. As I hesitate and my car stops, the dog leaps several feet away from the priest and almost lands on the car hood. It must know where the driver's side is, because it runs toward me and starts its frightening, nasty sounds again. The priest disappears into the church and my wheels spin out of the lot.

So much for revisiting places that were once tranquil and lovely but are now the land of defensive barriers, dangerous animals, and many dead ones. This town is not the one from my youthful days, its historic beauty camouflaged by concertina wire, chained beasts, and desperate distrust. The dead dogs are a suitable image for how Chamberino and much of New Mexico have changed, the towns and highways hiding something behind beautiful roadside altars and an eternal river, the sadness broken often by the echo of threatening songs. As the Southwest has changed and its highways have been built to cover every remote corner, the cost is paid by the dead dogs of the desert and their chained cousins.

I tell Ida this story as she steers toward Duluth. At the same time, I have been counting crows, their funny presence and lively demeanor replacing the memories of Chamberino. I am up to seven as we near Lake Superior—seven arrogant birds walking down the shoulder of the highway searching for food. I keep an eye out for road kills on this perfect road, but I don't see any. By the time we reach Duluth, I have counted nine crows. I may have missed one or two, but I don't think so. Nine crows hiking down the highway, scavengers on a clean road, birds who would love to feast in Chamberino, risking the live jaws of the wild.

But wait. I am wrong about the clean road. We come around the bend in the highway that gives us the first view of Lake Superior and there is a tenth crow picking at a McDonald's hamburger wrapper. It holds the bright yellow paper in its beak and flutters off into the grass as we go by.

Twelve Apostles

Conquest is the main theme in Southwest museums. The conquest of New Mexico by the Spanish dominates historical displays in the Albuquerque History Museum, located in Old Town, an area of gift shops created from the original settlement of the seventeenth century. I have visited several museums in Arizona, New Mexico, and El Paso, and they all feature displays on the Anasazi and their vanished civilization. Display cases of pottery, arrowheads, and weaving tools are lined up alongside maps of the Spaniard Juan de Oñate's journey north, along the Rio Grande. What often draws the tourist's eye are replicas of Anasazi dwellings, rooms that show what it must have been like to live in the pueblos along the river eight hundred years ago. I generally avoid these exhibits, preferring displays of southwestern art or presentations about wildlife of the area.

While visiting the Albuquerque museum for the first time in March 2000, I followed the signs that led to a huge three-room replica of a Spanish home of the early 1700s. The narratives in the display windows gave information on the antique furniture, artifacts that didn't interest me much, so I started to leave. As I passed the entrance to another gallery, I noticed an unusual display of armaments from the Spanish conquistadores, the loyal soldiers from Spain who did the dirty work in the name of the king and the Catholic Church. I avoided the glass window showing the various long swords and helmets and found myself in front of an old bandolier, a cartridge belt worn by the conquistadores to carry their gunpowder for their muskets. What caught my eye was the sign on the display—"The Twelve Apostles." Before reading on, I looked closer and wondered where the twelve apostles were and what they had to do with this bandolier. Someone may have mislabeled this exhibit or torn the sign off a painting of *The Last Supper* and stuck it here as some kind of joke. Where were Christ's apostles?

Then I read the description. The Spanish soldiers called the bandolier "the twelve apostles" in reference to the eleven tiny bags of gunpowder on the belt, plus the musket. Twelve weapons against the savages. Twelve apostles of faith and conquest against the people who refused to turn over their gold or lead the way to the Seven Cities of Cibola—kingdoms whose walls were supposed to be made of pure gold. Empty each apostle into the musket and deliver the gospel message. Declare your Christian duty against the pagans by carrying the twelve apostles into the New World. Fire and reload and there is one less apostle with each volley, one less Indian to subdue. The twelve apostles arrived with the soldiers, loaded into the muskets, and their thunder changed the history of this area, the words of the apostles carried inside tiny gunpowder cartridges worn around the belts of the Europeans. The twelve apostles crossed El Jornada del Muerto, in southern New Mexico of the sixteenth century, and survived to make it into the museum five hundred years later. The faith of these soldiers was eternal if I am to believe the version of history I was taught in school. I studied the decaying leather belt and strained to look through the glass into one of the eleven empty pockets of gunpowder. The display case held me back. I shook my head, but so what? This is the Southwest and here was a museum of artifacts from a history interpreted by those who conquered and settled it and have the final word.

The silence between words also dictates the symbols of conquest and what museums choose to exhibit. In the Palace of Governors' Museum in Santa Fe, a Xipe Totec figure hypnotizes me into staring at him for too long, and an elderly couple finally elbows me aside to get a look at this male deity from the Remojadar culture of the Vera Cruz, Mexico, region. The two-foot statue is dated around A.D. 400 and is of a standing figure with spread legs and outstretched arms, as if he is trying to scare something away. The Xipe Totec wears the skin of a virgin around his neck, the shriveled thing hanging there like a scarf, actually the remains of a young woman who was flayed and sacrificed for the gains of her male superiors. The pale face of the figure and his green, painted eyes glare at me, challenging me because I know what he has done. The silence of his cracked, clay face and a few missing fingertips from his extended fingers tell me he was found, preserved, and tagged as an engrossing treasure from a people his modern owners are supposed to understand. They dig up what the ancient earth offers them, whether beautiful or grotesque, and set it in glass as a statement that the past was so savage, there was no choice but to tame it.

When I walk out of the Palace of Governors, dozens of Indians are selling jewelry on the sidewalk, their black sheets spread out to hold rows of bracelets, earrings, and necklaces, lines of tourists pausing to consider prices lower than the ones in the fancy shops surrounding the square. The Indian vendors huddle in their blankets, a cold January wind slicing through the open plaza. Three young Indian boys, perhaps Navajo, watch the jewelry market from across the street and pass a bottle of tequila among them as they sit and laugh on a park bench, the low winter sun barely touching the frosty air at ten o'clock in the morning.

At the same time, the National Hispanic Cultural Center in Albuquerque presents something different from the latest view of pre-Columbian cultures or pueblo tribes. The Nuevo México Profundo exhibit features photographs from a book of the same name. The images chosen for display focus on the Hispano-Comanche culture of northern New Mexico and its colorful celebrations. Photographs like "El Comanche David, Talpa, 1966," and "Cuerno Verde y Don Carlos Fernandez, Alcalde, 1999" show Mexican American men dressed in native costumes as part of the matachine dances performed each year. The matachines are supposed to be Aztec in origin and are danced to portray the spiritual conquest of Mexico by the Spanish. The rituals captured on these photos dramatize Comanche raids led by the chief, Cuerno Verde (Green Horn), on settlements in the late eighteenth century. The men, some dressed as Comanches, others as soldiers, act out the play "Los Comanches," written in 1780 after Cuerno Verde was killed by the Spanish. It has been performed in northern New Mexico for more than two hundred years. The dance between the conqueror and the conquered remains timeless among people whose origins can be traced to the union of the two sides.

"Conversion de Moctezuma, Picuris, 1999" shows a small girl dressed as Malinche, the first Indian woman taken by Hernán Cortés, Spanish conquer of the Aztecs. She is converted and impregnated by Cortés and her son is the first mestizo, creating the Mexican race, while she remains the legendary interpreter and mistress of Cortés. In Mexico, the name *Malinche* is identified with betrayal. In New Mexico, she is seen as saintlike, almost equal to La Virgen de Guadalupe and representing the will of the Christian spirit to overcome paganism and convert every living soul in sight as part of making one world out of the old and the new. This is the oldest conflict between cultures of the Southwest and a struggle in which the mighty bandoliers of the twelve apostles left their mark. In the photo, the once proud Aztec emperor Moctezuma sits in a folding chair, mask on his face, and passively allows Malinche to tap him with her Catholic wand. This scene is played out every year in various towns in northern New Mexico, where these costumed rituals organized by Hispano-Comanche organizations depict the conversion of the Indians to Christianity. The story is a fictional narrative; historical documents never record a conversion by Moctezuma, who was killed by his own warriors when he was being held prisoner by Cortés. His killers were convinced their former king was helping the invaders destroy their world. Every girl dressed as Malinche wears a white veil, white dress, and white shoes—this vision of Catholic purity overpowering Moctezuma as he is led by Malinche into church where he accepts baptism.

Nuevo México Profundo could use the theme of conversion to sell its exhibit and book. Besides the series on the Comanches, two of the key images are "Batalla de Moros y Cristianos" and "Vuelta de la Malinche." The Batalla refers to the first play ever performed in New Mexico after all the native tribes in the area were officially subdued. Young children in Spanish costumes dance around a more passive group of their friends dressed as Indians, while the caption claims the reason for the play is to show the New Mexican struggle to teach the Indians "moral and political lessons" that would lead them on the road to Christianity. In "Vuelta," the same girl who converted Moctezuma spins in wild circles again, the powerful Malinche "awakening the spirit of Christianity in each matachine."

There is an alternative to Malinche and her Catholic victory over the Indians, but I do not find a single photograph in the museum to represent the other dance. It is made of Perejundia, a clown figure, usually played by a man in women's clothing, and a person dressed as a toro, the bull. They perform a ritual of mockery while the official history of conversion in New Mexico is acted out. Perejundia is raped by the bull to symbolize the brutal conquest of the people by the Spanish. This violation is carried out to show people another side to the story; the sexual rituals involving Perejundia and the bull depict the birth of the Indo-Hispano culture of the Southwest.

I am counting the number of photographs dealing directly with some kind of conversion ritual and do not notice the old man, until he bumps me and stands in front of one of the Malinche photos. "Excuse me," I say quietly and move on.

He is an elderly Mexican man with shoulder-length white hair tied back in a tail and wearing a long-sleeved white shirt with large stains under the armpits. He holds a cowboy hat in his hands and smiles at the array of photos on the walls. "This pretty young girl goes to my son's school," he tells me and points to the photo.

"Where does he live?"

"Alcalde. Have you ever been there?" He studies another portrait of the dancers.

"No, I haven't. I didn't know the Comanches had so much to do with these celebrations. Are there many groups in New Mexico that perform like this?"

The old man frowns. "We don't celebrate los Comanches. Our group honors the Lord and la Virgen. Somebody told me to come see this because it shows everybody how los Comanches want to honor God, too."

"Is your son in a group from Alcalde?"

The old man shakes his long hair. "No, Ricardo teaches high school and hasn't had much time to be in the group, but some of his students are." His name is Jose Saldivar and he says it is his first time in the new cultural center. His wife had a doctor's appointment in Albuquerque and will pick him up in the museum in one hour. Jose tells me more people should pay attention to what is left of "los Indios" and how Hispano Christian groups perform to show everybody that New Mexico is a good place for all kinds of people. Without another word, he wanders off toward sections of the display I've already seen. On the way out of the center, I ask one of the volunteers behind the welcome desk why the art center chose the word *Hispanic* in naming itself the National Hispanic Cultural Center.

"Nobody wanted the words Mexican American or Chicano," Jorge Castillo tells me. He is retired from his civil service job for the state and volunteers at the museum. "I don't know the whole story. I don't think the director is here right now."

"That's okay," I thank him. "I was just wondering."

I start to leave and he says, "Wait. I remember they turned down Mexican American because New Mexico art comes from many places, plus I think the word *Chicano* is too much like them." Jorge shrugs toward the exhibit.

"Too much like whom?" I stop.

He waves me closer, leans over the counter, and almost whispers. "It's a wonderful program, but lots of those people who dress like Indios are Chicanos from way back. Things aren't like that anymore. Beautiful pictures, but things aren't like that anymore." He straightens as other visitors come through the front door and I leave.

In 1519, searching for a way to recapture Mexico City after being defeated and driven out in a major battle, Cortés and his band of men waited for months outside the gates of the city. They held hundreds of Aztec warriors captive, torturing and killing many while strategizing on how to make their final assault on Moctezuma's people. During this waiting period, the Aztecs offered peyote and sacred mushrooms to the Spaniards for the first time. While the friars accompanying the Europeans were disapproving of such things, the taking of the hallucinogens was seen as a peace-making gesture by both sides. Within days of taking them and asking for more, the small group of Spaniards found the will and strength to make their move. The results in the final days of June included the killing of Moctezuma, the ransacking and burning of Mexico City, and the end of the Aztec Empire.

Alvar Nuñez Cabeza de Vaca wandered for eight years across Florida, Texas, New Mexico, and Arizona. He was the first European to see the Southwest and encounter many of its native tribes. As one of four survivors out of an original 1527 expedition of three hundred Spanish sailors, Cabeza de Vaca experienced great hunger and numerous illnesses and wounds, but he was the first to record what Indian life was like and to keep detailed notes on wildlife, such as buffalo, opossum, and many species of birds. He claims in his journals that what kept him alive was his newfound ability to heal sick Indians with his prayers and Christian faith. In chapter 53 of his journal, *Adventures in the Unknown Interior of America,* Cabeza de Vaca writes:

> Asked whom they sacrificed to, worshiped, and entreated for rain and health, the Pima Indians replied: a man in Heaven. We asked his name. Aguar. They said they believed he created the whole world and everything in it. How did they know this? Their fathers and grandfathers had told them; it had been passed down from a distant time; the old men knew that Aguar sent rain and all good things. We told them we called this deity they spoke of, Díos, and if they would call Him this and worship Him as we specified, it would go well with them. They replied they understood well and would do as we said. We ordered them to come down from the mountains fearlessly and peacefully, reinhabit the country and rebuild their houses and, among the latter, they should build one for God with a cross placed over the door like the one we had in the room and that, when Christians came among them, they should go to greet them with crosses in their hands instead of bows or other weapons, take them to their houses and feed them, and the Christians would not harm they (sic) but be friends. The Pima told us they would comply.

Many El Pasoans claim the first Thanksgiving Day in the United States did not occur in Plymouth Rock, Massachusetts, as is commonly believed. According to documented Spanish historical records, the first Thanksgiving Day is supposed to have occurred in El Paso del Norte, by the riverbanks in 1598, fifty years before the first Pilgrims arrived at Plymouth Rock and sixty-two years after Cabeza de Vaca came out of the wilderness and met his rescuers, Spanish soldiers coming up from Mexico. For several years, on the last Saturday and Sunday in April, the annual reenactment of Don Juan de Oñate's "First Thanksgiving" has been held at El Paso's Chamizal National Park. Oñate was the Spanish explorer who first crossed the Rio Grande at the future site of El Paso in 1598. His men carried plenty of supplies, and their bandoliers of the twelve apostles were fully loaded, since they had heard there were hostile savages in the land they were about to enter—Cabeza de Vaca's journals describing peaceful tribes were lost in Spanish bureaucracy, hidden among the thousands of documents being sent back to Spain. These documents described the progress of the expeditions and rumors about the City of Gold for which Oñate's men searched as they continued to encounter hundreds of uncoverted savages.

In March 1881, three Tewa Indians were hanged in San Jacinto Plaza in El Paso. The men who hanged them were members of Los Aguirres Posse, a notorious vigilante group of Mexican cowboys, ranchers, and adventurers who worked for several landowners in the area. Archives in the El Paso Public Library list the hangings but do not give a reason for them. An article refers to a group of photos taken at the mass hanging, but there is no trace of the photographs in the archives. A couple of library staff members help me dig through ancient files, but we find nothing further on this little-known incident.

In 1958 a sheepherder named Alfonso Martinez sat under a cottonwood tree in the Mimbres Mountains of northern New Mexico and noticed a piece of metal sticking through the roots of the tree. He dug down and found it was the hilt of a sword with a beautiful arabesque designed in gold. The whereabouts of the Spanish sword, made from Toledo steel, are now unknown. The weapon had lain in the ground for three hundred years.

From the April 23, 1994, *El Paso Herald Post:*
The Museum of History in Juárez, Mexico, received 112 Mexican archaeological artifacts from the United States through the Mexican Consulate in El Paso. Mexico had been asking the United States to return these artifacts for several decades. One of the items was described as a Paquime mummy. Marc Thompson, curator of El Paso's Wilderness Park Museum, said that although the mummy was from the general area called Paquime, it was not a Paquime mummy. He said, "It was from the nearby Casas Grandes cultural sphere—from a

smaller, Indian cliff-dwelling pueblo. It was buried under the floor of the pueblo, which was their custom." The mummy was that of a girl, possibly of toddler age, and dates to about A.D. 1200 to 1400. "It was in a private collection for many years and was donated to our museum," he said. In the late 1960s and 1970s, the mummy was on display in El Paso, but it was placed in storage after the Tewa Indians objected, he said. Finally, in 1994, the mummy and the other artifacts were returned to Mexico. While the Tewa Indians of west Texas hoped the Mexican government would return the mummy and the other items to their proper resting place in Casas Grandes, they were taken to a museum in Mexico City.

In Truth or Consequences, New Mexico, there is a tiny museum called the Geronimo Springs Museum. Besides displays of fossils and the skull of a mastodon, the museum houses an enclosed area called the Apache Room. It contains a life-size wax statue of Geronimo, as well as information on his life and how he avoided the U.S. Cavalry for decades, until surrendering in 1881. Other exhibits include the Hispanic Heritage Room, with a territorial gate and a complete altar behind it, and the Farm and Ranch Room, with tools used by early farmers and ranchers. The Ralph Edwards Room contains the story of why the town formerly known as Hot Springs changed its name to Truth or Consequences.

I drive through Truth or Consequences on the way to Albuquerque and think about Geronimo as I quietly repeat the phrase "The Twelve Apostles" to myself. In the name of Jesus Christ, the twelve apostles followed the highway I took from El Paso to Albuquerque and points farther north. De Oñate's men never read Cabeza de Vaca's journals, and many of them died in their search for gold. I look at the bandolier with its empty cartridges and imagine twelve tiny figurines of the actual apostles walking across the empty desert. Their trek would never be included in the history books we studied when we were growing up. I doubt the idea of a soldier's equipment being named after these first Christians would even interest a dance group in northern New Mexico; the defeat of the Comanches is a more colorful event to enact. It is the power of faith that named these weapons after those who delivered the word and tried to make all things come true for those who truly believed.

Conquest or discovery? I say both. And the discoveries haven't stopped. They are accelerated by what we learn when we witness the efficient manner of labeling and mounting them for public display and official history. The Twelve Apostles. I want to see a painting of Christ and his disciples at their last meal hanging somewhere in this tidy museum. As I leave, I turn for a final look at the bandolier. This was the last meal.

The Walls of San Antonio

The political and economic events that shook Mexico in 1994 surprised many Americans who favored passage of the North American Free Trade Agreement. As a city with close business and cultural ties with Mexico, San Antonio, Texas, reacted with worry over the Chiapas uprising by the Zapatistas, the devaluation of the peso, and the assassination of a Mexican politician campaigning for the presidency. San Antonio's politicians preferred the status quo, since Mexican stability helps south Texas. Despite being one of the ten largest cities in the country, San Antonio has always been hungry for outside dollars because it is one of the poorest cities economically, and its Mexican

American population has one of the highest illiteracy rates in the country. Despite its vast barrios, high crime rate, and clearly segregated sections, San Antonio has built a reputation as one of the premier tourist spots in the United States; it depends on American dollars and Mexican pesos to help it develop as an attractive place in humid south Texas. Former Mexican president Carlos Salinas de Gortari made several visits to San Antonio during his term. In 1992 he met President George Bush at the McNay Museum, on the city's prosperous north side, to sign a pre-NAFTA agreement. The city spent the nineties promoting itself to Mexico, poured millions of dollars into stronger ties with its neighbor, and made sure its attractive, historical sites like the Alamo and the River Walk kept bringing more tourists.

Mexico has a key embassy, a Cultural Institute, and a campus of its prestigious Universidad Autónoma de México in San Antonio. The San Antonio Public Library boasts that one of its busiest departments is the International Ties section, a center for information on everything you need to know about doing business with Mexico, including how to meet the right people. For several years, this department of the library had the highest number of public requests for information. Even the San Antonio city government Web site devotes several pages to a section titled "International Ties" and to its Casa San Antonio program. A San Antonio business owner can turn to the Internet to find the program's slogan, "Casa San Antonio: A strong team helping you to export." The promise of NAFTA and what it might bring to a new business is summarized by the city team: "Each year, over 100 billion dollars' worth of products and services is traded between the United States and Mexico. In fact, Texas is the largest exporting state into Mexico. Multinational conglomerates and small businesses alike are taking advantage of this opportunity. Export trade already represents a major market, and part of that market could be yours." The site encourages San Antonio businesses to work with city staff on setting up ties with Mexican officials and one of the Web site's buttons is titled "Your Offices in Mexico."

As someone who lived in San Antonio for six years, I was amazed at how the city and its people showed stronger ties to Mexico than did El Paso and its citizens. El Paso is right on the border and has to deal with the reality of illegal immigration, a cheap and legal workforce that commuted daily, and the uncontrolled growth of Juárez. The quality of life that is shaped by tensions on the border give El Paso a quieter, more sobering demeanor than

San Antonio, the fiesta town. Mexico and its citizens are not viewed by El Pasoans in the same light as people in San Antonio might view them. El Paso's isolation on the western tip of Texas places it a good six hundred miles from San Antonio and creates a totally different character. When I have spoken to people about my life in El Paso, I tell them a part of me feels I grew up in southern New Mexico, not Texas. I identify the Lone Star state with Austin, Dallas, Houston, and San Antonio, not El Paso. My hometown has more of a Native American Indian disposition, conquered long ago and trying to survive on little today. San Antonio is more aggressive and wants to celebrate the mother country of Mexico by identifying with the landowners and the families in governors' palaces. After watching events unfold in the aftermath of NAFTA, I concluded that San Antonio wants the Mexican middle and upper classes to spend time and money in San Antonio, thus redefining for Americans what it means to be Mexican—out with the domestic maids and gardeners in El Paso and in with the Yale-educated young Mexican and the cultural attaché. Trade and tourist initiatives are aimed at this new kind of Mexican rising out of the economic opportunities of NAFTA. While there are thousands of illegal immigrants living and working in San Antonio, they never seemed as visible to me as those in El Paso. San Antonio's desire to celebrate Mexico translates into notions of beautiful haciendas, margaritas on the River Walk, Mexican patrons at San Antonio Museums, and wealthy Mexico City businessmen spending millions in the city.

San Antonio's political clout on the border brought it the first NAFTA bank, which did little business in the first years of the economic pact between the United States and Mexico. The political events of 1994 in Mexico were not kind to San Antonio's plan to profit from NAFTA. During the months of debate leading to the 1993 congressional vote on the trade bill, the San Antonio Chamber of Commerce spent thousands of dollars on advertising in publications such as the *Wall Street Journal* and the *New York Times*. The ads proclaimed San Antonio the NAFTA city of the future and invited everybody to come and invest in what the city had to offer.

Having lived there in the midst of the NAFTA frenzy, I realized the city's aggressive stance toward better U.S.–Mexico relations, along with its desire to paint itself as a politically progressive city, has created a deceiving portrait of San Antonio. The thousands of tourists who line up every day to get into the Alamo are too busy enjoying themselves to understand that San

Antonio's attractive sites and political promotions are the profile city fathers want them to see. The River Walk, the Alamodome Stadium, and the Alamo are ironic symbols of how a city and its mixed population (60 percent Hispanic) can live in the past and present at the same time. These contradictions are rarely discussed, because heritage tourism brings dollars and jobs to south Texas, while some of the highest rates of poverty, youth gangs, and illiteracy in the nation continue to grow. Heritage tourism, as the art of repackaging and fabricating history for economic gain, saw a willing partner in NAFTA. San Antonio's dependency on places like the Alamo to keep tourists coming represents this romantic investment with the past. Its quest to be the premier tourist spot in Texas is carried out at the expense of the majority of local residents, who will never benefit from packed crowds at River Walk shops and expensive restaurants. Of course, there are many cities that highlight their history to get people to visit. San Antonio's advantage is that it is located in an area where monumental events involving Spain, Mexico, and the United States took place. The historical invasions and conquests left countless places to restore in the name of heritage tourism.

The Alamo, a world-famous monument that draws about four million people a year, is only one of several Spanish missions in the metropolitan area. The San Antonio Missions National Historic Park was established in 1978 to preserve the churches and protect 819 acres of historic sites and trails. Outside of the massive numbers of Alamo visitors, the city claims that one and a quarter million people visit the other missions each year. A tour of two of the other ancient sites on the Missions Trail showed me how a city with racial, criminal, and economic issues surrounds itself with the past while it tries to keep up with rapid political changes it hopes will cloak its problems. The U.S. Department of the Interior has done an amazing job of restoring the old churches and preserving the compounds of stone ruins, but the meticulous work has not kept the plight of a modern city from pressing on the walls; urban decay and the conveniences of modern living surround these beautiful landmarks. Two cycles of historic time play themselves out in San Antonio. On the one hand, this is a metropolis of segregated neighborhoods, one of the largest gang populations in the United States, and a local government obsessed with making San Antonio an upscale place to visit. On the other hand, there are the remains of the past, whose walls contain religious and social values that, in south Texas, have not changed a great deal in three hundred years. They give parts of the city a rustic, Spanish-style character as it fights to remain attractive in the midst of urban decay.

My wife, Ida, and I arrived at Mission San Francisco de Espada on a cool and overcast Saturday morning. The peaceful scene of the mission compound that greeted us two miles south of the freeway contrasted with our drive through some of the poorest neighborhoods in the city. Mission Espada is the most remote mission on the historic trail, which extends along twelve miles of the San Antonio River in the southern outskirts of the city. It was founded in 1690 as San Francisco de los Tejas and renamed Mission San Francisco de la Espada in 1731. A friary was built in 1745, and the church was completed in 1756. Crumbling, abandoned shacks and boarded-up icehouses line Espada Street toward the church. The exteriors of inhabited homes are decorated with pots of colorful plants, but all are enclosed within high wire fences. I noticed pit bulls and other mean dogs in several yards. As I drove past the last house, I waved to a group of four Mexican men who huddled around two rusting car frames. Even though it was only 10 A.M., the outdoor beer party was in full swing. A couple of the men paused in their drinking and watched us go by, one of them pointing at our car before taking another swig from his bottle.

When I turned into the mission parking lot, the first thing that caught my eye was the red graffiti on the Visitor Parking sign. A second, smaller sign reminded visitors to lock their cars to reduce crime. The semicircular red-stone walls of the baluarte (bastion), which was part of the main building, had two round holes in the corners. These were musket holes cut by the original Spanish settlers so they could lock the gates and shoot their guns at invading enemies. Farther down the baluarte were two larger slits for the cannon that used to defend the mission in the mid-1750s. The original walls also contained ramparts for the tiny garrison of Spanish soldiers. As the church farthest from the presidio of San Antonio and its sister missions, Espada had been a small fort since its founding. It was common for Apaches to attack the settlers and steal horses, cattle, and sheep. The strength of Espada as a fort was challenged in October 1835. Six months before the infamous Battle of the Alamo, Jim Bowie and James Fannin, two heroes of the Texas Revolution, made Espada their headquarters. With one hundred volunteers, they withstood an attack by two hundred Mexican soldiers.

I imagined a rifle sliding through the gun portholes of the baluarte to catch me in its sights. This area of south San Antonio was in the news a couple of months before when a gang of "taggers," young Chicano boys who loved to spray graffiti, were caught tagging a neighborhood bar. As the youths ran from the cantina, two irate owners in a van pursued them. One of the boys, Francisco Flores, was cornered by the proprietors and shot dead for spraying their business. He was fourteen years old and was chased into a field of weeds and tall grasses a couple of miles from Mission Espada.

To the left of the main structure, rows of crumbling stones spread into the compound. These were the remains of the original foundation. Rooms that once contained a granary, the convent, and tiny houses for the Coahuiltecan Indian inhabitants were slowly disappearing into the earth. Except for the tiny church and the main building, these rectangular outlines of old rooms made up the entire four sides of the mission grounds. Spanish policy in the New World dictated that missionaries build communities around the churches to resemble Spanish villages and their culture. This meant teaching the Coahuiltecans vocational skills such as blacksmithing, masonry, and carpentry. Their work and obedience are evident in missions throughout Texas. Local historians claim that if it weren't for efficient Spanish methods of teaching useful skills to the Coahuiltecans, San Antonio's unique Spanish-Indian character would not have emerged. Several tourist brochures refer to the successful creation of a large neophyte population among the area's original inhabitants. Historians may be the only ones to acknowledge San Antonio's mestizo roots. Today's promoters of stronger ties with Mexico prefer the modern Mexican, an almost-American who knows the power of money, and not one who is going to talk about his or her proud Indian heritage. After all, the lowest, most degrading insult someone in Mexico can receive is to be called an "Indio."

I entered the open doorway of the baluarte to be greeted by a National Park Service ranger seated at a desk. She was friendly and pointed out the slide show in the next room. Every few minutes, the taped commentary on the history of the missions was repeated. The park ranger explained the layout of the compound and reminded me that the church was still an active parish. Many visitors do not show courtesy when they enter a religious shrine and don't realize how much surrounding communities still depend on these ancient churches.

Emerging into the main compound, I felt immediate tranquility. In the midst of a city that is home to some of the worst barrios I have ever seen, I found one of its most peaceful locations. The picturesque church across the yard and the ancient layers of red rock lining the ground created an unusual beauty below an overcast sky. I was in an environment that was very fragile, despite having survived for two centuries and having a major city grow around it. The strict Catholicism introduced by the Spanish missionaries and the conquest of the New World created this mesmerizing circle of religious structures. The mission's ability to stand for centuries and sustain its contemplative atmosphere showed how well the Indians were forced to learn skills of masonry and carpentry.

At its peak in 1770, Mission Espada was home to two hundred Coahuiltecans. There was an old spinning wheel displayed inside the main building where the women made blankets. I tried to imagine the strands of color as they passed through the hands of the weavers. What was it like for the men to work in the granary and the carpentry, whose remains still stood under the live oaks? I wondered how many of the Coahuiltecans had voluntarily accepted Christianity when it first appeared on their native soil. How many were tortured and killed by the Spanish in the process of building the original mission? I have never seen the statistics in mission brochures or exhibits. Yet, as I walked under a huge oak near an old well, I was responding with a romantic notion that strikes many tourists when it comes to native people. When we enter breathtaking monuments of the past, we react to their beauty. When we daydream of what it must have been like to witness the world back then, we implant our twentieth-century character as we go back in time. If we have learned about the genocide involved in one race conquering another, we might study these ruins differently. Often their exquisite preservation dissolves our notions of searching for the real story we can't find in museum shop books. Life in these missions was harsh, but there are no facts printed alongside Park Service brochures that tell about the European diseases that wiped out hundreds of thousands, perhaps millions, of natives.

In *The Missions of San Antonio,* an official history sold by the Park Service, author Mary Ann Noonan Guerra claims the Coahuiltecans had "no particular skills or traditional tribal customs." This conclusion typifies the general feeling in San Antonio and the rest of Texas. Like many historians, Guerra concludes the Indians were the lesser culture because as a small, wandering tribe, they never had much to show anthropologists. They lived as a tribe for centuries before the conquest, so how could they not have values or survival skills? The mentality that says the Christian conquest introduced traditions to wild people is the same one that uses the missions to draw tourists. It is the reality that wants NAFTA profits to come to San Antonio, a city that often leads the nation in the number of reported drive-by gang shootings. Many of the eight hundred drive-bys in 1994, the year the trade agreement was passed, happened in the low-income housing projects and deteriorating schools located up and down the Mission Trail.

My thoughts were broken by the sudden blare of rap music beyond the park walls. The closest houses, separated from the mission by a high wire fence, were only fifty yards away. Two boys worked under the hood of a shiny black Chevy, their loud radio producing the rhythm to get the job done. As I moved toward the church, where Ida was taking pictures, the rap music diminished. To the right of the closed chapel, four women waited by a bright red sports car, as if someone was going to open the doors of the sanctuary. They were dressed for a church service, but no one let them in while we were there. An arched doorway dominated the chapel, with doors only five feet high. The park brochure said the arch generated speculation on how it was built. The decorative stones are broken in such a way that the lines do not match the design. It looks like someone placed one of the stones upside down as the arch was being shaped. According to the brochure, some people maintain the odd pattern to be a builder's mistake, while others think the inversion of the expected line gives it an oddly beautiful shape and myste-rious, spiritual connotations. Speculation about the arch focuses on Father François Bouchu, who oversaw reconstruction of the church in 1905, two years before his death. To the left of this odd doorway is a wooden cross that legend claims was carried by parishioners during a drought in the eighteenth century as they led a procession around the compound praying for rain.

A sign marked the convent, kitchen, and refectory, while another noted that Fray Bartolome García, one of the eighteenth-century friars who helped to develop the community, wrote a book inside the building. The manual was one of the few written in the Coahuiltecan language for use by the mission-aries in teaching the Indians. Today, no such language exists, though other signs in the park referred to the fact that a few descendants of the Coahuil-tecan mission community live around Espada. I wondered if the men at the morning beer party down the street were these descendants. We walked around the compound for another half-hour and saw the ruins of a school built in 1820 and used until 1967. The lone room was thirty feet long and barely fifteen feet wide. As we walked back to the car, the rap music rose in volume again, its rhythm making me think about which route I could take to find Mission San José, the other site we were visiting that day. We would hit heavy traffic as we followed the trail north toward busier parts of town. I paused by one of the ruins near the car where I spotted something carved on the wooden doorframe. It read "David R. loves Mary G."

As we drove up Espada Street, we passed the historical marker for the acequia, an irrigation canal. A reliable watering source was crucial to the survival of a new mission in a harsh climate, so the construction of an acequia was overseen by the Franciscan missionaries, who got the Coahuilte-cans to build seven gravity-flow ditches, several dams, and at least one aqueduct—a fifteen-mile network that eventually irrigated 3,500 acres of land. Spanish settlers measured their croplands in suertes, the amount of land that could be watered in one day. The watering system for the missions is one of the few things in the southern part of town that has outlasted everything around it, its ancient stones ringing with the sound of running water for hundreds of years, an engineering feat hard to duplicate today. The original Espada dam, aqueduct, and main ditch, or acequia madre, were built in 1731 and completed in 1745 and comprise the oldest system in the United States still in use. The entire acequia parallels the San Antonio River and runs for five miles between Espada and the dam, continuing to carry water to the mission, neighboring farmlands, and local residents who live on former mission land.

I turned toward Southeast Military Highway and the modern world came into view. The wide boulevard is one of the main congested routes heading south from downtown. We decided to eat lunch before finding the next mission, and Ida, who had taught at a college in the area a couple of years before, pointed to a popular Mexican restaurant. When I pulled into the shopping center, she expressed surprise at the number of new businesses. A Wal-Mart, a Luby's cafeteria, and several new dining places had been built. In their midst, a National Park Service sign gave directions to Mission San José. I couldn't see the tall dome of the mission, though it was less than a mile away. The clutter of neon signs and billboards blocked it from view and erased the tranquility of Mission Espada. For an instant, I was afraid I would not be able to find Mission San José; I felt disoriented because the area was no longer familiar, though I had driven through it when I used to work downtown. Our short drive from the peace of Espada into the real world made me hesitant to get out of the car. I thought about Fray García and what he may have instructed the missionaries to do about Indians who resisted the teachings of the Church. Where did they go when they ran away? I tried not to wander back to romantic tourist ideals. A car pulled in next to ours and woke me with its blaring rap music.

The familiar sound reminded me of the boys working on their car near the mission. I wondered if residents of these neighborhoods knew how far they could go before intruding on the solitude of the missions. The graffiti on park signs and the carved names on the ancient door showed some of them did not, though Catholic fear and guilt must protect most artifacts from complete destruction. It is one reason the clash of past and present continues in San Antonio. Its problems and rapid growth, common in many cities, become unique when the history of south Texas is reinterpreted for a foreign world through the tourist trade. This is done at the expense of citizens who have nothing to offer tourists; they are simply trying to survive in a segregated city where most of the Mexican and Mexican American populations hold low-paying jobs. Tourists do not visit the beautiful city for that. After seeing the poverty around Mission Espada and becoming nervous in the traffic on Military Highway, I concluded the missions use their religious icons and architecture to fight the disintegration around them.

In San Antonio, dual forces of time take on special significance because of the racial problems. I worked at a west-side arts center for four years and drove daily through a barrio of shattered tenement houses, nightly shootings and gang fights, and no effective city services. The defiant Chicano pride expressed by some of the center staff was never enough for me, because I could not get used to the injustice I saw on those streets every day. No matter how much art we could provide in the midst of great poverty, it could not ease the contradictions in San Antonio. Most of our programs at the art center were attended by middle-income patrons, some Mexican American and many Anglos. We had free concerts, poetry readings, and art exhibits, but they were rarely attended by the low-income inhabitants of Guadalupe Street and other neighborhoods around the center. City and state-funded arts organizations in San Antonio live in the world of Chamber of Commerce pride, not in the daily reality of public project housing, drug overdoses, and teen-age boys killing each other. We could program events to get kids from barrio schools into arts and crafts classes or offer them accordion lessons, but we could not bridge the gap between underserved communities and cultural offices that directed out-of-town visitors to the River Walk, the McNay Museum in the exclusive Alamo Heights neighborhood, or even the missions. In my four years of working on the west side, I realized that the city was the most segregated I had ever lived in. Closer ties with Mexico were not going to eliminate Texas's tradition of keeping "the Mexicans on their side of town," and new preservation plans for historic sites were not going to result in better public housing on the west side.

My mixed feelings at the missions acknowledged that San Antonio is one of the best promoters of civic and cultural pride. In the euphoria over the passage of NAFTA, new opportunities were dreamed about. Somewhere in the plans to promote investment over the new trade policy, the Chamber of Commerce must have found a way to include the mission trail and conveniently overlook the eyesores around it. There was heated debate over tearing down old buildings and dilapidated houses along the trail. Millions of dollars would be needed to create a historic corridor that would be lined with new stone and fresh landscaping. It would lead more tourists to the lesser-known missions and ease the lines at the Alamo. No agency had the money, and downtown merchants weren't about to divert business to other parts of town. Where would you house the hundreds of residents who would be displaced? You could tear down the barrios, but unlike wiping out the Coahuiltecan culture, you could not get rid of low-income families. In 1999 San Antonio city officials put together a detailed document called the Five Year Strategic Plan for the San Antonio Missions National Historic Park. It covers everything from fixing old trails to investing in ways to draw more people to the missions, but the plan doesn't address the urban nightmares and conflicts exploding in the streets around the churches.

Mission San José is surrounded, not by the poverty that surrounds Espada, but by the frantic pace of a city boulevard that roars past it. When I pulled into San Antonio's largest mission, construction fences blocked off portions of the crowded parking lot. Major renovation on one side of the compound and an extension of the parking area were under way. Mission San

José y San Miguel de Aguayo is an impressive, enclosed complex. Founded in 1720 by Father Antonio Margil de Jesús, a prominent Franciscan missionary in early Texas, the building has walls six hundred feet in length on the four sides. Three or four missions the size of the Alamo could easily fit inside. It was originally named for Saint Joseph and the Marques de San Miguel de Aguayo, the governor of the province of Coahuila and Texas at the time. The two longest walls contain tiny rooms in which the Indian population lived, at its peak numbering about three hundred inhabitants. Extensive crop fields and herds of livestock were nearby. Sealed doors line the walls every ten to twelve feet. These doors were made and installed by the Works Progress Administration (WPA) in the thirties. They are constructed of native mesquite wood and hung on replicas of iron hinges found during excavations in the thirties. The structure is enormous, and the entire compound was not completed until 1782. By the nineteenth century, it was known as the "Queen of the Missions." The thriving community defended against Apache and Comanche raids, the soldiers stationed there having taught the Coahuiltecans to use guns and cannons. Generations before NAFTA and San Antonio's drive to promote what it had to offer, Mission San Jose fell into disrepair. The San Antonio Conservation Society and the federal government began to restore part of the mission in the twenties and thirties, and the church was rededicated in 1937. In 1941 it was declared a State Historic Site and then a National Historic Site.

Two unique characteristics of the mission are the dome on top of the church and the legendary rose window. The dome, a media naranja (half-orange), measures more than thirty-nine feet across. It has a zigzag, chevron-type design, painted in imitation of the tile work of Puebla, Mexico, and built with concrete of pulverized stone, sand, and water in 1778. The bright dome gives the mission a colorful Moorish design. The rose window, the only opening on the south wall of the sanctuary, is ten feet in length and has intricate Gothic designs on its frame. During the Feast of Pentecost each year, it was the site where the host was shown by priests to gathered worshippers.

The church is also one of the few frontier missions with intricate statues and sculptures carved over the doors and the keystone entrance. San José with the infant Jesus stands above the front window, with Saint Dominic to his right and Saint Francis to the left. Above the carved oak doors is Our Lady of Guadalupe, patroness of the Americas. Saint Joachim and Saint Anne, parents of Mary, the Mother of God, guard each side of the entrance. These features, combined with the traditional Renaissance details of the other buildings inside the enormous walls, give San José a different atmosphere from the other missions. Hundreds of years after its founding, it is alive and takes visitors back in time, its mighty walls insulating its ancient atmosphere from a city that now wants to make certain every aspect of its heritage is spruced up and presented to a willing tide of tourists.

At San José it was not possible to find the peaceful solitude I experienced at Espada, where I counted seven visitors. Here more than one hundred people were going in and out of the stone granary building and walking in small groups around the churchyard. A souvenir shop in one of the buildings was doing a brisk business, selling everything from postcards and miniatures of clay missions to Indian jewelry. The city regularly holds traditional music concerts, plays, and holiday events in the small amphitheater. *Los Pastores (The Shepherds)*, a Christmas pastoral play, draws thousands of people every December and has been staged at the mission for more than two hundred years. Well-kept flower gardens behind the church, with begonias, hibiscus, and blue maze lining the worn columns of Gothic arches, extended for a hundred feet. Originally constructed out of red brick, the double row of twenty arches was added in 1860 as part of the expansion of the mission into a seminary. The two-story building below the arches contained small rooms connected by spacious galleries, and the second floor held the former living quarters of the missionaries. Other rooms were the refectory, an armory, and a special room set aside for costumes for the Indian dances.

I read in the park brochure that the colorful costumes were kept under lock and key, used only when the missionaries allowed the Coahuiltecans to stage festivals. These were held to replace mitotes, the religious and artistic festivals of the natives. The friars called these ceremonies pagan because they could lure the Indians back to their "life in the brush"—the phrase the author of the booklet used to describe the pre-mission period. In modern Spanish, the word *mitote* means a lie, an untruth, or pure gossip. I guess only the authors of these brochures know how to tell the truth. Even though an earlier passage in the brochure decided the Coahuiltecans had no culture, the section on San José acknowledged the musical talent of the Indians. One report of the times stated, "Most of them are able to play a musical instrument, some the guitar, others the violin or the harp." The Coahuiltecans also made their own guitarlike instruments from gourds, and abundant replicas of these were for sale in the shop.

A stream of people moved through the entrance and across the compound with its trimmed lawns and massive live oaks. This place was large enough to keep traffic sounds on Military Highway at bay, though any second I expected to hear the boom-boom of rap music. The mission was close enough to downtown San Antonio that many visitors spilled over from the Alamo crowds. They would not arrive with blaring car radios, carve their names in the wood, or stand in fenced-in yards by crumbling shacks to stare as you neared the next historic point on the trail. These tourists seemed to come here in awe and with respect for San Antonio's sacred spaces of its past, the strong walls that welcome them to experience "the West" and its captivating history. Many people carried expensive cameras, and the ones who looked like San Antonians were conservatively dressed as if going to mass on Sunday. Some of them entered the church and did not emerge immediately. These visitors to San José would fit nicely on a Chamber of Commerce brochure or a city Web site.

The park service and the city created a world within a world at the massive San José site. The last section I visited was Pedrajo's gristmill, named for the Franciscan designer who built it with Coahuiltecan labor in 1780. The square blockhouse sits half underground on the north side of the compound. A grove of live oaks and pots of Spanish dagger cactus surround the pit where water used to fall from a height of ten feet into a stone reservoir. The force of the water supplied through the acequia turned a wheel that moved the grindstone. Wooden stairs lead into the lower section of the mill. Images of manual labor, hard stone, and water running over the acequia came to me. As Ida and I strolled through the beautiful park, I pictured hundreds of Coahuiltecans kneeling on the pews inside the church. The odor of incense and the sound of Latin prayers chanted by the priests filled the stifling air. I watched the Indians work in the mill and haul bags of grain, their families lined up in the yard to receive the peck of corn, meat, and tobacco missionaries passed out on Sundays. Despite my cynicism based on the facts of cultural conflict, I gave in to my imagination and idealized notions about the missions. At the same time, I couldn't forget the decay and swift changes outside their walls.

San Antonio's location made it the center of Spanish authority centuries ago. Spain exercised that power by destroying the traditional life of native people forever. The later Texan inhabitants revolted against Mexico's rule and changed the course of history at the Alamo. Today San Antonio profits from its history because Texan pride calls for it. The media's declaration that the nineties was the decade of the "Hispanic" compels Mexican Americans and Mexican nationals to flock to the pleasant side of San Antonio, not the Guadalupe streets or the rows of tenement houses. With or without NAFTA, San Antonio will attract millions of people annually. They will come from Mexico, Japan, Germany, and other parts of the world. The lines at the Alamo prove it, and the compound of Mission San José welcomes more and more visitors each year. The expansion of the parking lot underscores that fact.

As we drove away, I looked back at the sturdy walls. They were taller and thicker than the crumbling ones at Espada and I did not see any graffiti or signs of vandalism. I pulled onto Roosevelt Street and headed toward downtown. An abandoned drive-in theater, with a huge screen frame and hundreds of speaker poles lining acres of tumbleweeds, stood north of the mission. Its rusting corrugated metal fence had wide gaps along its length, making it a tagger's paradise. You could fill a book with the many colors and letters along the fence. Fray García's Coahuiltecan text came to mind again. I wondered how many pages it filled and what colors of ink were available in a time when language and its symbols were as enduring as the red stones of a protective faith.

Part Four

Which of My Hands on the Pictographs?

Which of my hands belongs here, rubbing the surface of the rock wall to see if history has been thorough in hiding everything that happened? Which color will my fingers scrape off the rough surface, the moisture of my fingertips seeping into the surface like a thief stealing color from the pictographs? More than three thousand paintings to choose from at Hueco Tanks; the gravity in my shoulders pulls toward Cave of the Masks, the opening in the earth I enter. I was afraid to climb up here, but the sign warning me about rattlesnakes gave me permission to climb without thinking surprise will quicken me or make my hands into fists.

I dreamed the Indian pictographs last night, the symbols on the rocks coming to me for the third time in the two months since I visited the ancient site. The dreams are colorful and I am pointing to the arrows, masks, and horses with my fingers, the tips coming close to the rock but never touching them. There is usually a child with me, but these children know nothing about the prehistoric Jornada Mogollon or the Mescalero Apaches. They depend on me to show them where the red paint has defied the heat of the desert sun for centuries.

The scientist said the most sensitive portion of the skin, at the tips of the thumb and index fingers, is treated by the brain in much the same way as the most sensitive part of the retina. Is this why the Jornada Mogollon people chose colors for painting from available minerals—so they could see and feel at the same time? Hematite and limonite gave the masks their red hue. Various shades of ochre produced red and yellow; carbon and manganese were used for black, the charcoal smeared on their palms and faces, streaks of ash announcing the next meal. White clay and gypsum yielded white paint, while oxides of copper created green and blue. Bending over the fields and harvesting with sore hands, making sure something was saved to enhance the mineral hues. Perhaps vegetable dyes and substances to bind them—their own urine, egg yolk, plant juices, and animal fats. The scientist says to use the tips of the thumb and index finger. The paints were applied with brushes made from yucca or human hair or by blowing pigments from reed or bone tubes. Finger painting.

I passed this way many times and depended on my booted feet to warn me of danger. When I bent down and touched the white tips of the thorns on the ocotillo, the sharp moment was held inside memory—the time I gripped the dead hawk in my trembling hands as feathers and blood covered my wrists, tiny ants falling out of the crushed body. I dropped the bird and ran, rubbed my stained hands on my jeans, trying to forget the sound behind me.

There are few words in my dream of the pictographs. I depend on the rough images to speak for me as the mute world of dreaming communicates something that has taken a lifetime to learn—the language of silence and the speech of the eye where what I see rings from quiet image to quiet cliff to silent humans. We observe the masks on the boulder, the long serpent stretching across the rock ceiling with black walls from old fires, holes in the rock cupped out by the Mescaleros who camped here before attacking another ranch near El Paso del Norte. On the other side of the coiled reptile are red triangles and pointed stars that look like thin fingers outstretched beyond the outcropping to reach for something no longer there. I find these things in my dream and have stood before these red cliffs so many times that it is not a strange land. The jagged boulders and sheer walls rise out of the flat desert to eliminate time and defy the desert's need to erode. By sheer luck, and of course by asking the park ranger, I find the Quetzalcoatl mask with its plumed serpent on top showing jaguar teeth. It is painted above a narrow ledge usually off limits to visitors on the tour. I crawl on hands and knees and balance myself about twenty yards below the drawing. It is as far as I can climb, sweat pouring down my face, the grove of cottonwoods and salt cedars in the canyon below waving in the hot wind as I think I am going to fall. I spot the leaping horse under the huge head of the painted snake, an image I have seen before. When I come to see them for the first time, I have already been here, and the language of my silence has been ringing for years, my hands reaching out without touching anything.

When the scorpion fell off the ceiling and landed on my bed, I was asleep and only discovered it in the morning when the dead thing lay stiff between my shoes on the floor, the shoelaces on the carpet laid out in a strange pattern I once saw in the life lines on my palms.

The observers study our movement and conclude the first stage of exploration is not under voluntary control. In our vision, our eyes move automatically toward the target and focus on it before searching out its identifying optical features. When we touch, an unknown object is grasped and instinctively oriented toward the hand, or the hand itself is oriented over the target surface, what we want to take, what we devour in our touching, until everything has come into contact and we are part of it or it is part of our open moment.

Desert vision means ignoring the cactus and its dangers and concentrating on the moving figure. Who is he? What does he have to do with my outstretched arms? Are the electric fences on the border humming with traffic, shocked hands charred and fallen in the sand? Look at the two vultures in the distant sky. Did someone say they have radio transmitters on their wings?

What do I do if I have visited this site only once in real life, but have known it from birth? One image has yellow flower petals painted between the red triangles as if the Mogollon man found a new substance to mix in his bowl, adding color to bring full clarity to my discovery. Flower petals on walls beyond the horse and rider who attack the site with a violence the people have never seen before: I know this image. It is all over the desert. In the Cave of the Masks is the geometric figure of a goggle-eyed Tlaloc, a rain deity who was beneficial and destructive and was associated with sacred mountains. Rain so rare in the desert. Sheer cliffs rise 450 feet from the desert floor, their massive, volcanic outcroppings rarely seen in this part of the Chihuahua. Tlaloc stares down at me, designs and colors of rain and abundance alive in the symbols that includes a turtle, a rain altar, a solid mask, and a mountain sheep. Black, red, and yellow colors shimmer off the sure hands of the artist. The canyon at Manchito had the figure falling off his horse, several arrows finding their mark decades before the last graves of the defeated warriors were dug. When I point out these things to the quiet children in my dream of the pictographs, they turn to look without speech. Perhaps anything their infant tongues might shape has already been burned on the walls. They look at the designs closely, wonder about the eyes in the oblong mask that glares at us, their questions of silence finding space in what I sense is instinct and what I go after out of curiosity, my hands folded quietly around a notepad and pen.

There is a moment in writing the poem when the world lifts and you see it, like the touching of language upon stone left in the rain too long. The photographer finds the dry husk of a dead beetle stuck on the wooden door of her studio and is delighted at being able to shoot it with a macro lens. It is the same desire filling the image and emotions of the poem, where existence is tightly wound around the precise thing that is no longer yours. When you capture it, you actually let go; the beetle will be gone a few minutes after the photographer puts down her camera. A black hornet enters my study through a torn window screen and falls onto a sheet of paper like a jewel that has lost its wings. It hits the paper with a mild thud. As I type the words that guide the flowing river onto a new stanza, the hornet flies away and leaves a tiny black speck on my white paper. When I finish the short poem and go to print it, I insert this sheet and wait. The line about the red faces painted on the walls is laser jetted over the hornet's gift, the black grain it left not quite fitting over the word *heat*. I hold the printed poem to the light and search for the hornet, but it has disappeared from the room, the moment of finishing the poem the exact second it found the tear in the screen and made its way out. Who is to say what the residue from the hornet's body is doing in my poem? It may be part of the language, or it may be mistaken for smeared ink, the printer not quite doing its job. Something has touched the poem. When we pay careful attention to what enters our creative sanctuary, we choose the things we want to keep. Rivers, dreams, and incidents from childhood that, in time, mean more to the poet than to the reader. Is the dry husk of the beetle floating in the wind? What if I had crumbled the stained sheet of paper into the wastebasket and flattened the hornet with my notebook? How many poems have I missed in this way? Not every waking moment deserves language or vision. Who said that? A confident poet after four or five published books? What does he know? There is a bend in the Rio Grande north of Hatch, New Mexico, that is one of my favorite areas along the river. When I visit the state, I go there to see the brown water rush around the great bend as it disappears into thick groves of cottonwoods, salt cedars, and mesquite. My lookout point is the highway bridge that crosses the water and commands traffic to keep going; the scenic spot rushes by unless you know it is there. The image and the poem about the river become a whispering recitation in my head, but I don't bring the poem with me when I stop there. I know where to look to summon words I composed long ago. When I drive to the bend years after first writing about the river, I surrender the poems I do not write in my return. I will miss some of the details of having left a long time ago— my choice of what I allowed to go with me filling my notebooks and typed pages as I listen to the buzzing of a yellow jacket, this larger insect hovering close but unable to get in through the screen.

The intelligent researcher tells me that in writing, as in stone tool manufacture, the dominant hand's performance is micrometric, rehearsed, and for the most part internally driven. The performance of the nondominant hand is macrometric, improvisational, and externally driven. What about the third hand that is always there, resting on my shoulder as I write, its invisible push reminding me I have not turned to look over my shoulder in many years?

I looked up from the back of the room, and the poem on the blackboard was being copied by the old poet, my teacher whose wrinkled wrists traced the last few lines to make sure I would see them. The sunlight broke through the classroom window and settled on the dusty board. I didn't believe it, and the poet who tried to teach me held out the chalk and waved it in the air so we would listen. The last couple of lines revealed how the poet crossed the road with gloved fists in his coat pocket, trying to get to the other side before something pushed him from behind.

Who sees with their eyes when the poem arrives in a Joseph Cornell box, its words and stanzas pasted into a vision bouncing off the sides of the box? His parrots are my parrots, the one I used to have for a pet as a child. My aunt nicknamed me Perico—Spanish for parrot—because I loved to imitate the sounds of the bird. The long wait for Cornell's parrots began forty-five years ago when my parrot died. Who blinks at the objects when the poem already contains them—antique hairbrush, a crushed golf ball from 1923, the label from a long-extinct Bulldog beer bottle, two pairs of eyeglasses, sewing needles glued on one box wall, layers of what look like the scaly fins of fish lining the box to make room for the parrot on its perch. What are these objects in their chosen frames? We have objects from our past we can never forget, their appearance in our writing reminding us they are not lost, only waiting to be taken off the shelf. When Cornell searched bookstores and pawn shops, I searched my mother's house and the arroyos behind it washed out by rain. Fossils in rock; *Look* magazines from 1956 stored in the garage; shriveled skeletons of lizards under tumbleweeds, their ribs and tail the size of toothpicks broken in half; a 1943 Lincoln penny; one arrowhead of dull green-and-red flake; a rusted tobacco tin; and pink plastic hair curlers my mother wore in 1952, the year I was born. Who fills the box and writes the poem with an old ballpoint pen that skips and finally runs out of ink? When Cornell walked the streets of Queens, he did not know what he would find. His search took him farther and farther away from his childhood, yet it brought him closer to the moment when he was born. One collage is a doll's face peering out from behind thorny branches and twigs, her black eyes gazing out as if the world is never going to end. Are they tumbleweeds from my desert? Sharp and dry branches of mesquite break off and roll miles in a dust storm, only to be found by small hands and mounted in a box where a turtle shell looks out from behind the thorns, the reptile body inside having disappeared long ago, the empty shell becoming a crown of rough jewels, the invisible head of the turtle appearing to the boy, now and then, an early attempt at collage broken in a pile of discarded toys in the garage where there is nothing left but birds. They talk to me as if they know who I am, their feathers breathing inside the boxes to point to streets I have never walked, their squawking meant to pull an electric cord to start a fan, turn off a radio, or flick on a bulb in the box. They are perched in the dimension Cornell demanded when he pulled chaos out of pawn shops, used-book stores, garage sales, and the junkyard of hidden desire. These parrots repeat words that might release them from the boxes so they can land in a tree of their choice. Once I heard a loud squawking outside a friend's house and he pointed to a palm tree and the wild parrot on top he claimed had been coming there for fifteen years, the old thing returning to the neighborhood each summer, then disappearing for the rest of the year. Cornell's parrots reappear in the postcards and the boxes that never leave the shelf, the decades of being fed by the hands of strangers alternating between years of dark feathers and years of light. Which poem encounters this construction toward the moving birds? Which words, silent or reverberating with speech, re-create the need to glue things together, Cornell's magic turning basements into kingdoms of clairvoyance, aviaries where he knew what was going to happen decades into the future? When the desert rain stopped and the arroyos opened, my small fingers made it through the deep water as I gripped the bones in one hand and the fossilized shell in the other. I studied them and thought I saw the body of a fish take the underground river and open it to the curious world, its empty boxes of desire waiting for my hands to fill them and change the course of the muddy stream.

Once, hiking alone in the moonlight at Manchito, I saw something cross the path ahead of me. Thinking of snakes, I stopped, but its slow pattern revealed the beauty of the tarantula, its determination to get across the road slowing everything down, until the oncoming darkness gave it the gift of invisibility, my brief urge to reach down and take it disrupted by fear of touching it. I waited for other tarantulas to follow it, but the white dirt of the night revealed nothing. In the morning, I pulled out the heavy rock I stashed in my knapsack.

The first signs I ever saw when I got lost were the two painted red hands on the rocks, their long, ancient fingers outstretched toward the sky as if the painter was pleading to the flying powers to let him live and see and not show the color of death. Farther into the canyon at Comanche Cave, I notice a panel of what appears to be dancers, painted in white. The men are playing instruments, someone is riding a horse, a man is chasing a girl, and the dancers are in a row. This is a historic painting of a Mescalero Apache victory dance: the flying wind after death and victory, the color of blood and the white color of the future. The guide tells me it was probably painted between 1820 and 1840 when Mescaleros raided in the area. Someone has painted "1849" over some of the pictographs and my hands want to erase the date of the earliest Anglo sign at Hueco Tanks. Nearby, the cool water cistern is marked in Lula Kirkland's handwriting with "Watter Hear." Kirkland, a photographer, was the first person to document the pictographs in 1939.

I have not visited the Abo ruins in twenty years. I get out of my car and gaze at what has been done to them during that time. The ruins of the Catholic church stand tall and eerie across the low juniper hills. At least two steeples are still standing, though their immense red rocks look like they are going to fall at any moment. There is now a park ranger station and museum, with carefully manicured trails leading around the site. I spot a sign that wasn't here twenty years ago—"Beware of Rattlesnakes." Stay on the Trail. Rains and thunderstorms have followed me all the way from El Paso to Albuquerque. On a whim, I turned off I-35 and headed east into the southern edge of the Sandia Mountains. The sign for Mountain Air, the town up the road from Abo, was still there and took me back twenty years when I was in graduate school and drove here with two poet friends. We were in the creative writing program and were very competitive. My two friends were from New York and had never experienced the Southwest. We went on weekend drives, which gave me a chance to show them New Mexico. We camped near the ruins, but in 1978 they were fenced off and closed to the public. We slept in a tent on a windy hill and stayed up most of the night because of the cold and the fear of what? Bears? Mountain lions? We didn't know, but I felt uneasy the whole night, knowing we were probably sleeping on top of an unexcavated mound that was part of the Anasazi pueblo Spanish explorers found in 1620. Now, as I walked around the larger excavations and got to see the great kiva for the first time, I recalled those old feelings of companionship and innocence. Here I was, with an elderly couple and a young girl, the only other visitors, walking where my friends and I slept two decades earlier. I stood before the kiva and read the sign telling tourists not to climb down. In recent years, I read a great deal on the Anasazi and their mysterious disappearance from the Southwest. The more I traveled in New Mexico, the more obvious it became that our curiosity about these people has transformed itself into a lively tourist trade. I looked down at the dirt and tumbleweeds piled in the circular chamber of the kiva and wondered if these places were still sacred because we wanted it that way for our enjoyment. The red church to my back dominated the pueblo, as had the friars who ruled over the people, destroy-ing their native religion and forcing them to build missions in the name of Christ. This is the old story of conquest, and I add nothing new to it, but what about the slavery, the hard labor, and the thousands who died building these places? How long could they continue to worship in the kiva when the enormous church towered over it and overshadowed their beliefs? Here was the tourist and native son returning to a beautiful, isolated place he had always liked, but how could I bow before the church, or even the kiva, without questioning how our interpretations of the past serve the present, realign the historical record, and bring southwestern states plenty of tourist dollars? As I looked across the crumbling courtyard of the church and read the brochure telling me that most of the pueblo remains unexcavated, I knew the camp-out my poet friends and I experienced twenty years ago may have been a more honest way of acknowledging this place than coming here to be guided through the ruins. As I walked through the rooms behind the church, it started to rain. I smiled at the young woman who was going in and out of every room, a look of fascination on her face as she studied the red walls. The elderly couple put hats on and ran into the room where I stood. Of course there was no roof, so we were getting wet. "Have you seen most of the ruins in New Mexico?" The man asked me. His wife looked at me through her sunglasses. "A few," I answered. They nodded as if this was what they wanted to hear and quickly left. As the rain came down harder, I decided to go back to my car. I hurried through the corridors that surrounded the kiva and paused in the rain. I looked down at the hole and saw my two friends and myself inside our tents about fifty yards from where I stood. Twenty years ago, the kiva lay hidden and we claimed we heard noises above the wind. It was past midnight and the two of them had fallen asleep. I peeked out from my sleeping bag and looked toward the ruins of the church. In the cold night, the silhouette of one of the steeples could be seen. I stared at it and heard something. I thought it was a coyote and buried my head in the sleeping bag. I couldn't sleep and looked out again an hour later. The darkness of early morning hid the ruins from my sight and I stared at the hills that rolled up to our campsite. I reached out from my sleeping bag and grabbed a handful of dirt outside the tent. The ground felt warm, though the air was very cold. To this day, I remember the warmth of the ground, as if we had cooked over it hours before. I fell asleep with the fistful of gravel in my hand.

The scientist advises me to look at the extreme orderliness and predictability of individual handwriting and says this is due to the mode of generating and controlling the movement. He wants me to take a good look at what my hand is actually doing the next time I write. For a good laugh, he wants me to slow down the rate at which I sign my name—by about half—and see if I recognize my signature. What about slowing down the poem and my familiar handwriting in my journal? What if the poem is composed on the computer? How do I slow it down? Where do I sign my name? How many drafts do I throw away? Did something whisper which ones to keep? How many Folsom point arrowheads can I collect and get away with it? The guide says those arrowheads usually mean mammoth and giant bison bones are nearby, the hunt of eight or nine thousand years ago having taken place nearby: the tired hunters dragging their prize into the cool shadows of the canyons, signs of a successful hunt blossoming in red, yellow, and white all over the caves. Yet the scientist says handwriting and animals weren't always around for me to depend on and dream about. He tells me the Early Archaic style of pictographs at Hueco, which he dates from 6000 to 3000 b.c., consists of curvilinear and rectilinear abstract designs, no words and language from the hands, except for the comb designs and parallel wavy lines of the period. He says it is hard to guess at the meanings of the oldest drawings, the kind most seldom found at Hueco. There are no animal or human depictions in this earlier style, he concludes. No hands, no palms, no open acceptance of a story in writing, only the geometric eye and heart burning into the red rocks to pronounce things are going to happen with both open hands and closed fists.

There is a hand. We call it memory. It closes, opens, and speaks. There is a river that flows and lets us cross time and time again. Everything depends on this river. There is mud and the barbed wire border we can't touch. There are people and mountains and canyons, cottonwoods and snakes, and hidden hands watching it all, tired of rubbing the rosary as if the river is going to lower its level and drowning victims are going to walk out of the slime to embrace their loved ones with dripping green hands.

I ran my fingers over the fossils I found in a washed-out arroyo, the rough spiral of shells embedded in the rock to make me see with my fingers, trace their resting place to the sharpest vision of the pictographs in my dream— the moment I see a wrinkled hand drop the pine needle brush into the pot of red paint and wipe drops that fell on the fingers across the rough surface, three smeared lines blossoming on the rock as words I learn in my sleep.

Why hands? Why not the feet or the brain that has never been touched by a finger? What about the masks at Hueco? The largest concentration of Indian painted masks in North America, more than two hundred, is at Hueco Tanks State Park, twenty-five miles east of El Paso. The masks are significant because their designs and the religion they represent influenced the rest of southwestern art. You can see the masks in every Hopi kachina you buy at a tourist shop. The expert tells me the face is the "gateway to abstract thought" and he says nothing about hands, how they think on their own when I cross out several stanzas in the first struggling poem. In putting on the mask and in painting them on the high cliffs that remain inaccessible, the masked dancer becomes the intermediary between the human and spiritual world. What about the hands holding the rattles and beating on the war drums, the sweating brown fists that pound the knife into the screaming elk?

What about the hands that take off the mask after the dance to re-create what has been seen on the rocks? What remains for the naive visitor—the mask on the jagged surface or the hands that painted it? Which appears first in the dim light of the cave—the face or the arms on the emerging body, sunlight outside the cave washing everything into shattered boulders that can't be touched.

The researcher concludes: Hominid hands did shape tools for striking and piercing and cutting, did ignite and control fire, did fashion clothing and habitation, and did domesticate animals and cultivate plants. But with their hands and developed brain and greatly increased eye-brain-hand neural circuitry, hominids may well have invented language—not just expanding the naming function that some animals possess but finding true language, with syntax as well as vocabulary, in gestural activity.

Now there is no reason to understand my poem, simply to hold it without cause or complaint. That day, I felt the intricate patterns on the wall and one or two edges cut my fingertips, but the drawings and the words were there. I pressed harder and saw blood appear across a pigment of color in the old creation. I had climbed up here to give the ancient site what it had waited for—a sense of hope as I ran my open palm over the map hidden on the wall, the horse and rider leaping over the sun to wave fire in their legs, make me say two or three words about the rock I was trying to hold up with my straining hands. The very first rule visitors are given on a sheet of paper as they enter the park: "Do not touch the paintings on the walls."

The Underground Heart

I stare at the enormous opening in the earth. It appears ominously around the corner of the stone wall. Several people go around me, ignoring the cascading flock of birds above them. A couple bumps into me as they descend the asphalt trail into the cavern, the cave swallows flying over their heads to disappear into the darkness below. For a moment, I mistake the birds for bats, and the error reminds me I have not been to Carlsbad Caverns in twenty years. Thousands of Mexican free-tail bats will not emerge from their home until late evening. Until then, the swallows swing back and forth between the cliff walls, their nests hidden in the pockmarked layers of sandstone. An occasional beep echoes above my head, but I have never heard a large group of birds be this silent.

I continue down the narrow trail into the huge opening, the asphalt path meandering back and forth, and I feel the magnetic pull in my legs when I enter the earth—a brief, scary feeling that brings a familiar rush to my legs, the careful awakening I have felt upon entering a narrow arroyo as well as the one time I approached the rim of the Grand Canyon. I am going inside the ground to visit a space that might redefine my sense of landscape—familiar desert terrain of an outer world that has grown distant after two decades of living elsewhere. The sweet smell of bat guano permeates the cool darkness, its odor adding to the attraction of the entrance, telling me there is something in the heavy air down there, an underground presence that has drawn me to the Chihuahuan Desert to enter a submerged territory of caves with their man-made comforts. The crowds of tourists mask my private search for the kind of light needed to accept the fact that the desert region I knew as a young man is gone forever. Many of the visitors to the caverns are awed and left wondering how this underground world can exist in the middle of nowhere. It is a common reaction among many first-time visitors to the Southwest, who assume the hostile desert doesn't have much to offer. To those who have driven their motor homes across the desert for the first time, this is really "nowhere." For those of us who know the Southwest but can't remember the difference between a stalactite and a stalagmite, the darkness below is a fresh, mysterious retreat into a past reshaped to entertain millions of people and perhaps to educate them to geologic wonders few national parks offer.

Carlsbad Caverns is one of the more isolated sites in the U.S. park system and lies twenty miles north of Guadalupe Mountains National Park. First-time visitors from other parts of the country are surprised to find such hidden beauty in the Chihuahuan Desert of southeastern New Mexico. Once they spend a full day exploring the caverns or hiking and camping in McKittrick Canyon in the Guadalupes, they see that the largest desert region of the United States contains unique national parks. To understand how environmentally fragile this region is, you must look at Carlsbad Caverns and Guadalupe Mountains National Park as one complete ecosystem. Their isolation and the harsh conditions of the desert may never make them as popular as Yellowstone or Yosemite, but like other parks at the turn of the century, the caverns and Guadalupes are vulnerable to thousands of people and vehicles that come through each year. It is not easy to get to this remote section of south-central New Mexico. To accommodate visitors, an amusement park atmosphere has been created at the caverns—unfortunate but necessary in drawing six hundred thousand people here every year—with the result that thousands of limestone formations in the caves have been destroyed by the simple touch of people's fingertips. At the end of the century, the Southwest is no longer empty, and the park system does its share to make sure more people keep coming. Big Bend National Park in south Texas remains a popular, though rugged, wilderness area to visit. Carlsbad Caverns is available for the less ambitious. Together they are bringing more and more tourists and recreational vehicles to west Texas and southern New Mexico.

I saw these changes on my drive from El Paso, 150 miles to the west. The June heat wavered at 100 degrees when I passed Hueco Tanks State Park on Highway 180, east of the city. The red cliffs of this old Apache watering hole used to be covered with graffiti. I recall my high school days when drinking there was the thing to do—drive twenty miles out of town with your buddies and a six-pack of beer. None of us cared that vandals were defacing many of the ancient pictographs at Hueco Tanks. As I drove past the park thirty years later, guilt came easily. I loved the desert when I lived in El Paso, but as a native, I had no environmental concerns. There was no such thing back then. We were too busy growing up in a vast landscape that could never change. I wandered the desert as a teenager, wrestling with branches of ocotillos and cottonwoods, climbing great landslides of rock to reach a cluster of prickly pears at the top. This is how my early poems came to me—rising out of arroyo solitude, not from a genuine ecological awareness.

Now I passed Hueco Tanks and drove into something that shocked me out of my high-school memories. Highway 180 was crowded with a five-mile stretch of auto junkyards. Endless rows of wrecked cars glistened in the distance as I counted eight separate auto-salvaging businesses. In the sixties, this road was empty and a straight shot to Carlsbad. Today, it was a deposit for everything that had gone mechanically wrong in El Paso and Juárez. I sped past sign after sign announcing cheap car parts and finally entered the empty desert. I had not driven this road since 1978 and remembered a rough, four-lane highway with little traffic. No sooner had I left the junkyards behind than I ran into a stretch of road repairs where the state was widening the highway. A line of cars slowed my vehicle. We moved at twenty miles an hour, a tall parade of motor homes and vans in front of me making it impossible to see where the construction ended.

It had never been this difficult to get out of town. The highway between El Paso and Carlsbad is normally one of the most isolated in west Texas. Rolling dunes and low red cliffs spread in all directions. The Chihuahua is a stark but beautiful desert with creosote bushes, mesquite, and prickly pears. Along 180 they grow in clusters, with miles of nothing in between. The Carlsbad region of the Chihuahua contains an abundant growth of lechuguilla cactus, also known as agave and what the Indians of the area referred to as mescal. You could come across mescal plants on the surface of the hills around the Caverns. Was there a message in mescal being a hallucinatory extract of lechuguillas, growing where the earth swallowed you and revealed unusual things deep below the surface?

I tried to spot familiar landmarks as I came upon a section of road that rose in elevation and curved through several low canyons. I had never forgotten this stretch because of the thousands of tall yucca plants that grew for the next few miles. Their density was still here, one of the few places along my route that had not changed in twenty years. When I came around the last curve of the yucca forest, Guadalupe Peak, a hundred miles away, appeared. As the tallest mountain in Texas, it dominates the desert at an elevation of 8,749 feet and is visible from all directions, never disappearing from the horizon. Guadalupe Peak is the lower end of an ancient reef formed more than 250 million years ago. The great mountain is the protruding Capitan reef and the caverns its underground body—a world formed from the timeless breath of enormous forces that left the peak as a visible sign there is something growing and expanding under the known desert.

The traffic tie-up cleared and I made fast progress. I was busy staring at the mountain when I suddenly passed Cornudas, a ghost town of a few crumbling buildings on the north side of the highway. As it zoomed past, I remembered stopping for gas there years ago. Thirty miles later, another image from the past flashed by. The only other roadside town is Salt Flat. I ate there on my last visit to the caverns. I had no idea it was the last trip I would make in the desert before leaving the Southwest for good. I slowed down and saw the "Open" sign over the tiny restaurant, just as it was in 1978.

It took another two hours to reach the base of Guadalupe and begin the long ascent around the mountain. Its sheer cliffs rose into the sky like ancient castle walls. I was home and yet I was far from my forty-nine-year-old relationship with the desert and its power that came from above and below. National park brochures claim there are more than two hundred caves in the Guadalupe Mountains, most of them unexplored. As my car slowed to a crawl on the steep road, the mountain to my left could have been the great, sealed entrance to many secret chambers. The ancient reefs say experiencing the desert is not complete until you hike it in the living air of the sun and descend into its hidden country under your feet. The mountain brought back the memory of a young writer wandering the lighted trails of the caverns twenty years before, deep tunnels and black entrances echoing what he would write once he climbed back into the light.

I left Guadalupe Peak behind and closed my eyes at the wheel for an instant. The whirl of a bat tornado lifting out of the ground opened them and I tried to recall the last time I saw thousands of bats in flight. I blinked and saw myself at the age of twenty-six, wanting to take something out of Carlsbad Caverns—a rock, a chip of aragonite crystal from the Green Lake Room one mile underground, even a postcard from the gift shop. I tried to recall a souvenir from my visit two decades ago, but I had none. As a native, I knew a great deal about the desert I could see all around me, but practically nothing about the broken, subterranean earth. I had never considered the desert's hidden geological forces to be the prime source for the way the canyons and arroyos of home were created. Could I act like a park tourist with no history here and simply enjoy the magic of the caverns? I had chosen to see them because the increasing use of national parks in the West says a great deal about how people relate to vast wilderness spaces, immersing themselves within them in short, intense visits. Whether visiting the Grand Canyon or Yellowstone or the more challenging and isolated Big Bend, tourists face certain limitations because of their sheer numbers and the caution necessary in traversing the wild. A majority of the caves and deep chasms in Carlsbad Caverns are sealed off from the public, with man-made trails making it safe for passing, but the caverns are different from other national parks in the way they have been transformed into a submerged playground that takes advantage of their unique natural wonders.

When I crossed the New Mexico state line, colorful signs to the caverns appeared everywhere. Turning off the highway at White's City, I noticed several shops and museums that had not been there before. Indian jewelry and rocks were the main items promoted on signs and in windows. The six miles to the park entrance wind through a beautiful canyon of yuccas and limestone cliffs, the narrow two-lane road climbing gradually until it ends at the huge parking lot. Rows of parked cars flashing in the sun and families leading their kids toward the museum buildings resembled a scene from a busy amusement park. Cries of excitement from arriving visitors echoed across the low cliffs that surround and conceal the massive opening in the earth. The high plateau at the entrance offers an impressive view of the Guadalupes to the south, the distant horizon beyond the mountains visible for what must be more than a hundred miles.

I was disoriented from the driving as I stood in the Visitor Center line to pay my six-dollar entry fee. The brief welcome and cave orientation given to groups of fifty by a park ranger helped. She told us to stay on the lighted paths and to use the metal handrails as much as possible so that we didn't slip and fall on the rocky surface. The restrooms and the handy lunchroom at the bottom were built seventy years ago for park staff and visitors who used to descend 276 steps to the bottom, do their jobs or tour the caves, then climb those 276 stairs back up each day. The ranger explained that now the elevator shoots people to the surface in less than a minute. Then she said, "Anyone with chewing gum? Get rid of it. No gum in the caverns."

It wasn't until I descended into the darkness that I felt my highway fatigue leave, to be replaced by the sense that I was very far from the outer desert. I could no longer see the swallows darting behind me or the lime-stone rim pockmarked with their nests. The entrance was a pinhole above my head, the descent a black tunnel in front of me, the pull in my legs a cool grasp from the interior. The smell of bat guano intensified as I followed a line of people who "ooed" and "ahhed" at the emerging wonders of the panoramic formations, the humidity and smell reinforcing the feeling of sinking and letting go toward a place I had never been.

We passed the main bat cave two hundred feet down and I expected a ranger to be there to tell us about it, but the lighted sign pointing out the area where thousands of bats lived stood alone. I put on a jacket before beginning the mile-long walk through the Main Corridor, which started at the bottom of our quick descent. The average year-round temperature inside the caverns is 56 degrees Fahrenheit, and I immediately felt the cool contrast from the heat on the surface. The line of tourists slowed as we got our first look at the immensity of the caverns. The Main Corridor is a steep and narrow passage, historically important as the natural opening where the first explorers discovered the caves.

Another lighted sign said that an old metal ladder, hanging across the chasm from our viewing point, had been propped there since 1923 when men like Jim White probed deeper into the unknown. White worked for a group of businessmen who were mining the caves for guano and is credited today as the official discoverer of the main caverns. These earliest visitors entered the caverns in a large bucket that was lowered by cable down one of the mine shafts, lanterns and candles their only source of light as they dropped into unexplored levels of this new world. Two people could ride the bucket elevator on each 170-foot trip. The trail where this famous ladder hangs was built in the 1920s. Ancient wooden steps beyond the ladder were visible in the walls that ended where the original entrance had been sealed long ago.

At five hundred feet down, Devil's Spring is one of the first enormous formations to display the wonders of the park. Rock towers, high caves and hollows, and barely visible columns of limestone were washed in shades of blue, orange, and white—an intricate electric lighting system buried throughout the caverns. The guidebook explained that stalactites hang "tite" to the ceiling and stalagmites "mite" reach the ceiling if they grow enough. Hundreds of them decorated the distant ceiling in Devil's Spring and rose from pools of water on either side of the trail. Later I would see the largest stalagmites in the Hall of Giants, some reaching heights of sixty feet and diameters of ten feet.

The occasional sound of dripping water echoed around me. I listened as the drops rang from an unseen source and faded away, and I tried to find where they came from. The pools are ecologically fragile and easily disturbed by the slightest touch or movement. The trail I followed ran between several pools of light green water, the rocky cups that held the liquid illuminated by dim lights around their rims. I inspected several pools and each was perfectly still, not a single ripple or splash disturbing their glassy surfaces. A family of four passed me and I heard the young boy talking to his father about how Miss Carlton, his science teacher, had told him what to watch for. The boy was thrilled—a common response I observed all day amid these natural creations. The excitement of the children emphasized how the caverns have been tamed and dressed up to a point where the young feel carefree and can have fun interpreting geologic puzzles with their runaway, though educated, imaginations.

Several people went by with cameras and flashlights. Most of the crowds kept together and followed the line, but as the tour progressed, young kids ran down the trails on their own. As we went farther in, the deep pits and black fissures added a sense of danger to the enjoyment of seeing the caverns. Not every parent was making sure their kids stayed back from the edge of marked trails. Even though recent park service records showed a slight decline in the number of yearly visitors, Carlsbad Caverns remains a haven for the young and old who want to learn something different about the earth. This crystal environment takes them far from the deer, bears, and crowded campgrounds of other places they have visited. Beyond the thrill of being inside a cave and wondering what lies behind those enormous pillars and unreachable black chasms, there was a lot to discover here. I overheard one girl tell her father about speleothems—formations with common, petrified popcornlike clusters clinging to the walls everywhere I looked. The girl's father leaned on the railing and arched his head way up, trying to focus on the complex lines, jagged points, and colorful, twisted shapes. Imitating him, I strained my neck to gaze up as far as I could, and the distant ceiling released a feeling of vertigo. The chambers coiling upward seemed to defy gravity in the way the massive columns of limestone hung by thin, solid threads.

Carlsbad Caverns is unique among the country's national parks. Despite the Disneyland atmosphere created by the colored lights and tour signs, the caves are an exciting place to learn about little-known geologic processes. The fragile environment of the caves, the endless darkness, and the odd sense that there is something unknown beyond the lighted trails makes for the kind of day that can't be experienced outdoors above ground. The best example is the Big Room. At fourteen acres, it is one of the largest underground chambers in the world. It takes more than an hour to walk the circular route through this area with its popular sites like the Bottomless Pit, the Hall of Giants, Rock of Ages, and the Painted Grotto. The level trails and easy accessibility from the high-speed surface elevator make the Big Room an ideal place for tourists who can visit only briefly.

The Big Room is also the best example of how the current use of Carlsbad

Caverns increases the long-term risks of exposing fragile environments to so many people. In the Hall of Giants, a mesmerized crowd encircled the Giant and the Twin Domes, gigantic stalagmites that rise more than forty feet from the floor. People stood along the metal railings and gazed at subtle hues of green, orange, and white limestone deposits that ran down the slick sides of the domes. The formations resembled slices of my mother's ice cream cake, their huge, smooth sides fields of frosting on that dessert. The awe and wonder on the faces of the dozens of visitors gave these colossal structures a sweet and soothing character. Our curiosity was drawn by a pattern of helictites above the Giant Dome—strange formations on cave ceilings and walls that appear to have total disregard for the law of gravity. These thin calcite crystals grow downward, sideways, and in circles, their sharp edges contrasting with the massive stalagmites below.

A sudden, metallic crash boomed over the crowd. An elderly woman lay sprawled on the asphalt trail, one of her legs entwined in a camera tripod. A photographer helped her up, the embarrassment on his face clear in the dark passage. He had broken one of the park rules banning tripods on the narrow trails. I had seen him earlier trying to place his equipment for a proper shot of the domes. The woman was okay, but the commotion drew a ranger, who spoke quietly to the photographer and got him to pack his camera. Moving on, I bumped my head on the low ceiling of a short tunnel that led toward the Temple of the Sun. As I exited the rocky tunnel I caught a teenage couple kissing passionately, their bodies leaning against the railing and blocking the flow of people out of the tunnel.

I squeezed around them to reach the Bottomless Pit before taking a break in the lunchroom, the rest area with bathrooms 755 feet below the surface. After several hundred feet of flat trails and glowing structures that loom beyond the roof of the cave, a twisting section of railing leads to the Pit overlook, the scariest part of the tour. The Bottomless Pit is actually 120 feet deep, but its sheer drop makes it appear to fall to the other side of the world. Its name makes it one of the most popular stops. I was surprised that only a handful of people stood at the fence covering the railing. The park service had illuminated the entire area in spooky blue lights that increased the pull of the deep I felt in my legs. I could not make myself stand at the edge to look down, so I gripped the railing and stood a few feet back. The pit must be at least fifty feet across, and its murky canyon is like a magnet.

A teenage kid behind me turned to another. "Look! Suicide Point!" His buddy pushed him, and the kid's sneakers squeaked loudly on the stone trail as he braked and gripped the fence. They cackled and moved on.

Two teenage girls giggled, bent over the railing, then quickly backed off in silence, one of them holding her open hand over her mouth. They hurried after the boys and one of them said, "Jenny said she kissed Bill right here."

I tried to read the sign describing the pit, but three people blocked my view. As I turned the corner, a small boy pushed against me. His mother grabbed him by the arm and pulled him away from the railing. "No!" she hissed. "I told you no! Let's go find Jimmy!"

The boy started crying. "I want to go to the bathroom," he sniffed at her. As she lifted him in her arms, she slipped on the moist trail. She grabbed the railing to keep from falling and joined a man a few yards away. The nervous energy of these people made me change my mind about reading the history of the pit and learning how it was discovered and explored. I headed for the lunchroom, a good one-mile trek away.

There were few people between the Bottomless Pit and the lunchroom, making the eastern side of the Big Room the quietest to explore. The last major site before the rest area is the Painted Grotto, a vast cut in the chamber that surpasses our descriptions of beauty. The natural chemical processes form a mix of colors that are amplified by the artificial lighting, creating endless shadows and colors on the walls. One stalactite after another rains down from great heights, each curtain of rock creating new dimensions of beauty. You keep looking behind the last one and there is another, the layers of the grotto vanishing to a fine point of darkness that is perhaps one to two hundred yards distant, but which can never be reached as it moves farther and farther away. The rock canvas embraces fallen boulders, pools of clear water, and unknown passages carved millions of years ago, restless seas drying into miles of caverns that remain unexplored to this day. Protruding mounds of stalagmites drape themselves beyond sight, their solid, receding march making the Painted Grotto the underground heart of a living ecosystem—a shimmering core of geologic transformations that thrust landscapes outward, toward their fate as rugged desert to be fought over, inhabited, and parceled out for human use. While the outside world changed and struggled to prosper, this deeper and older territory continued to evolve, its geologic processes unseen by the naked eye and incalculable in their impact on the world above.

I found a viewing area with a bench and sat down. No more running kids, scolding parents, fanatic photographers, or teenage couples blocking the narrow passages. Had I really expected an empty park for quiet contemplation in the middle of tourist season? A few people passed as I wiped the sweat off my face with my jacket. This was it, why I had come. The untraceable sound of dripping water, the distant echoes of voices, and the smell of the unknown surrounded me. Loneliness set in as I breathed the dampness and acknowledged I had never been here before. I could arrive at this resting place only as someone who had disappeared from home decades ago, my ignorance of the extent of the underground heart and its blood passages to my past lost somewhere in the booming darkness. The immeasurable power of the desert reentered my heart, coming at me from underground, an unexpected source of solitude and possibility. I thought of the naturalist and writer Richard Nelson and his book *The Island Within,* about his adventures on an isolated island in the Northwest. Contemplating what he has been trying to learn about home and his inner self, he pauses in his treks over water and writes, "I see nothing except an unblemished glory of blackness. Not one light anywhere. The island is alone, unburdened, self-contained, possessed of the rarest kind of purity. I wish for a way to reach out and touch it, tenderly, like a face in the darkness."

These caverns were certainly lit, and I could not be alone in an attractive park like this, but its massive formations, so close and so distant, told me I could go only so far in exploring their "rarest kind of purity." There were guard rails and guided tours and Jim White's ancient ladder to lead one along, but no man-made system could approach the "unblemished glory of blackness" that remained between stalactites and grottos, filled dead-end passages to unexplored rooms, and generated a gravitational pull that could take a visitor away. In the most optimistic sense, there are beats of this underground heart we are not supposed to hear and never will. Perhaps we believed the only way down had to be carved by our hands, so we could arrive at the edge of the Bottomless Pit and admit that our limits of exploration are right there and should stay there. These days, what possesses the rarest kind of beauty is rare itself. With the fight over digging a radioactive waste dump only miles from these caverns, moments of being unburdened in the desert of possibilities are vanishing fast.

I sat in the Painted Grotto, contemplated how far down I had come, and realized this place stood still in time as it was slowly changed by the constant arrival of the curious—the users of national parks who were going to get their money's worth, then take the elevator back up to their air-conditioned RVs and say they had a great time. No darkness is allowed; they keep visiting by the thousands. I looked up at the faraway ceiling and wanted the unexplored earth to open before me, yearned to witness a stalactite break off to crash into a secret opening unlighted by park electricity. The impact would be monumental, last eons, and start new growth in the blackness that might tell me I belong down here, hundreds of feet down in the fissures of prehistoric creation, as much as I belong upstairs climbing the Franklin Mountains or walking along the Rio Grande. I wanted to measure a quarter inch of epsomite needles to find the millions of years it took to create that quarter. The cluster of needles would dart from aragonite trees, petrified beyond the reach of passing visitors to wait for me. I fantasized defying the rules by breaking off a soda straw from the formation on the other side of the railing and rolling it in the moisture of my palms. Taking the bright pink thing in my hand would give me the energy to count the miles and decades it took to get here, thanking these eternal processes I did not really understand for allowing me to bypass the public park atmosphere and be able to take them in. Clutching the forbidden would help me understand that returning to Carlsbad Caverns was necessary in accepting the unforgiving terrain outside, along with the danger of the deepest cave, its darkness marked off, lit up, and mapped.

I came here because time passed without me knowing everything I should have known about the desert and its secrets. One visit to the caverns would not take care of being gone or the knowledge I lacked, and besides, a national park set up for human use makes room for a limited amount of freethinking and speculation about where we belong. The ride comes first. Yet this tiring excursion convinced me that encroachment meant not only an active park, but also a need to be in these caves to listen to their echoes. Without paying attention to the silence here, I could never accept the desert as one burned by the sun and cooled by these chambers. Searching for silence in a public park has its extreme limitations, but these caves with their cool dampness and majestic moonscapes were the place to search, because there had always been two atmospheres in the hard landscape where I grew up. My years of hiking canyons and arroyos had been a long, roundabout way of getting to the other half of the Chihuahua—the underground heart that was patient in its darkness. This quiet, arterial terrain was inhabited by bats, microorganisms, families enjoying themselves, and by the lone witness of time. It took coming here for me to see this, even to appreciate the park's public use and to respect the blackness of those walls beyond my reach.

Carlsbad Caverns is a strange place. The average visitor can experience the kind of fun one has at a place like Disneyland or else take the timeless, geologic dance of rock seriously. Either way, invisible planes of time and ancient architecture lie here for anyone to find. The guidebooks warn visitors not to touch the formations, but for every inch of violated rock, there are millions of feet of undiscovered, living geosystems buying time in a public system.

More sweat poured down my neck and a couple passed by hand in hand. An elderly man held his grandson and pointed to something on the ceiling. The joys that hundreds of families shared today reinforce the argument that the environmental risks are worth the rewards of having national parks. I talked to Ranger Tom Johnson when I left my bench. He stood at the edge of the Painted Grotto, where I asked him about the changed cave environment. He said the construction and maintenance of trails, the blasting of elevator shafts, and the millions of visitors have changed the ecosystem of the cave over the years. Since the majority of the trails are self-guided, vandalism is a problem. Between 1985 and 1993 thousands of small formations were broken. He also described how rubble from the blasted elevator shaft is slowly being removed from the cave. Under the rubble flowstone, rimstone dams and other natural features have been found intact, and the park service is working to clean and to slow the damage from so many human bodies entering an environment where they are foreign invaders.

"Are your shoes clean?" he asked, pointing to my feet.

"What?"

I looked at my shoes as he explained how people track mud over the flowstone and into cave pools—soil from the outside world that does not belong down here. Volunteer workers have identified these areas and have removed as much of the dirt as possible. For many years dust and lint have been accumulating. By the 1990s it was hanging in large globs and covering fragile surfaces. It had never occurred to me that lint from people's clothes could damage the caverns. The accumulation was holding moisture and slowly dissolving cave formations. Ranger Johnson said an estimated eight to ten pounds of lint are left behind each year.

"We could make sweaters out of the lint, sell them in the shop, and make some extra money for this place," he joked.

"Do people break off pieces of stalagmites and take them?" I had not seen anyone touch the formations but figured the temptation is great.

Ranger Johnson shrugged. "It happens, but we don't catch people very often. It's hard to break pieces off. I think the main damage is from people simply touching fragile things and leaving bacteria from their fingertips on the surface. It may take years, but the pure state of this place gets contaminated. I did pull a kid out of a pool once. He was okay, but who knows what he left in that natural water."

I thanked him for the information and took my break. The fast-fried menu in the lunchroom must certainly accelerate the level of contamination down here. By the time I ate a bland sandwich and watched the crowds in the cafeteria, I was ready to return to the top. The operator joked with his passengers as he hit the button, telling us that the modern elevator fell all the way to the bottom years ago—not the best thing to tell a car packed with tired people. Before we reached the surface, he admitted he had been joking. People looked at one another and shook their heads. It took exactly one minute to shoot seven hundred feet up to the Visitor Center, and no one in the thick steel tube we rode in felt the rapid ascent. Before we exited, the operator said it was 108 degrees outside. I could feel the scorching heat inside the museum and took off my jacket. Even in the air-conditioned lobby, I knew it was very hot outside. It was close to five P.M. and I heard someone say the bats were not flying until after seven. I spent two hours in the museum bookstore, which contains some of the best titles on natural history I have seen—everything from the history of native people in the area to books on New Mexico and desert wildlife. I found field guides to every Southwest animal from snakes to amphibians, scorpions, and tarantulas. There were special guides to New Mexico's wilderness areas and books on the Navajo, Apache, and Hopi that I had not seen before, including hard-to-find titles from university presses. Of course, rubber bats, videos and books on bats, bat T-shirts, stuffed toy bats, bats on cups, and bat decals also filled the place.

It was past eight before anything started to happen in the outdoor amphitheater. I joined a group of about two hundred people who stayed for the event and listened to a ranger give a short talk on bats. I noticed the absence of the swallows I had seen upon entering the cavern. Had they sensed what was going to happen and gotten out of the way? I could not see the opening because of the stone wall between the entrance and the amphi-theater. The ranger told us a variety of the fifty species of bats in the United States have been found in Carlsbad Caverns, but the majority are the Mexican free-tailed, so named because they spend much of their lives in Mexico. Unlike on most bats, part of the short tail of this bat is free from the membrane between its legs. It is small, weighing about half an ounce, and has a wingspan of eleven inches. The colony at Carlsbad is made up primarily of females, who give birth to their young from June through July before migrating in October to winter in Mexico. At its peak in 1936, the colony numbered an estimated 8.7 million bats. The number decreased over the de-cades to approximately 200,000 in 1973. In 1996 there were about 190,000, up to 350,000 each fall when the young were flying. Scientists think that DDT has been the primary cause of the decline in the population and there is concern that someday Carlsbad Caverns could be completely empty of its magical bat population.

I was pondering these statistics when excited voices made me look up. At first I thought the cave swallows had returned, because the flying things in front of us looked like birds. Then it became clear that the lead bats were coming out. I focused on the sky above the entrance as the emerging bats quickly grew in number, a whirlwind of rushing creatures shooting into the air at great speed. Several people shrieked as the escape began; it seemed as if everything underground was pouring out of the earth, as if what I had desired down there was being released. A wavering cloud of bats stretched toward the south, and as they moved away, their growing distance seemed to carry my earlier perceptions with it. I thought they would rise and scatter in every direction, but the thick mass stayed together and moved away from the mountain, a swirling presence that did not want to be near the hundreds of amazed, sweating faces below. A low humming sound intensified but did not last very long. I forgot to look at my watch, but someone later said the flight took twenty minutes.

I sat stunned at the evaporating signs of the bats and my journey was over. People stood to catch one last look at the quiet entrance now clear of bats. A few stragglers flew out and disappeared across the evening sky. I did not leave my seat because the cave had not only been emptied of bats but had cleared itself of the inner space of my earlier contemplation. Whatever I had seen and concluded about the darkness down there did not fly with the bats. It belonged hundreds of feet below and would stay there. Perhaps next time I would pick up where I left off and explore a part of the caverns I missed this time. The bats were gone and this was now a total, complete desert. It always had been as it had waited for me in the midst of welcoming thousands of people every week. Guadalupe Peak and the Painted Grotto would be the extreme extensions of a desert that demanded I redefine what home meant to someone who had been gone for years and needed to descend to be told whether tremendous movements of desert and place had already left the native behind. By following the trails to the bottom, I had found a place to begin, an open space, cool and petrified below, yet warm and moving as I came up.

The oncoming darkness filled the Pecos Valley between the park and the Guadalupes and was brighter than the blackness I had encountered below. The beginning stretches of a red sunset filled the arroyos to the south as the purple mountains fought to keep their light. For an instant, I wanted to go back down into the caves, but they were closed. I wanted to carelessly run down the trail and listen to the echo of the human visitor losing his voice and his years away from the region. In his need to flee, the gravity of great, enduring rock and limestone opened a passage to a ground that could never be abandoned but only opened after many years and numerous attempts at returning. The caverns could not be left behind by anyone because they had always been here, reef upon breaking reef expanding after billions of drops of water insured there would be a world to discover. I followed the line of departing bat watchers but was not really leaving. Familiarity was the highway and the yucca forest of fresh air that filled the red sky of a desert evening. But my house was the piercing fissure that dropped deep under the red sky to show me there is more than one way to get home.

Hazardous Cargo

My car idles on the shoulder of the two-lane road, about a hundred yards from the entrance to Caldwell-Briseno Industries, a thriving solid-waste disposal facility in Sunland Park, New Mexico, ten miles northwest of downtown El Paso. I can't see what lies behind the metal fence; its threads are tightly wound together, and barbed wire runs along its top for hundreds of feet. I think I see mounds of dirt beyond the barrier and warehouse buildings spread throughout, but the long row of diesel trucks blocks my view. Eight of them are lined up at the gate, waiting to be checked off and allowed to enter and deposit whatever hidden cargo they are carrying. The entrance is reinforced by a guard house, where three men in uniform stand inside the glass watching the slow-moving parade of vehicles.

I sit in my car with the windows closed because of the exhaust from the trucks. The plant is near the Rio Grande, and Cristo Rey, the mountain with the statue of Christ at the top, looms over the area, its brown slopes two miles away. A friend in El Paso told me about this place, hidden from view because acres of cottonwoods, salt cedar, and other river vegetation surround the perimeter of the dump site. Most people don't know of its existence or what is left here after empty trucks roar away. As I count the vehicles, two more pass me and get in line, and I wonder if anyone ever questions why so many loud trucks turn into this area off the main highways on the west side of the city.

I wanted to see how a waste dump so close to town operates, perhaps even talk to some residents of Sunland Park, but my plans are cut short when a white, four-wheel-drive van screeches to a stop next to my car, the blue-and-green Caldwell-Briseno logo painted on its doors. The uniformed driver, decked out in sunglasses and blue baseball cap with the logo on it, stares at me until I lower my window. He lowers his passenger side window and I see he is Mexican American.

"I'm sorry, sir, but you can't stop your car here," he says politely.

"I was just driving through and wanted to see all the trucks," I tell him above the roar of the waiting line down the road.

"You can't stop here." He looks over his shoulder as a radio squawks inside his van. "Turn around right here and you can get back to Doniphan."

"Isn't this a public road?" I point toward the street that goes past the gates.

He looks at me without answering, his brown face with its thin, well-trimmed moustache glistening under his cap. "Turn around right here, sir. No unauthorized vehicles are allowed to stop here."

"Okay," I say and wave good-bye. He pulls forward so I can make a U-turn before another truck arrives and blocks me on the shoulder. I spin around and head back toward town. Four more lumbering, weighed-down trucks churn toward the facility before I reach the main road out of Sunland Park. Before I get on Doniphan, it hits me. None of the trucks in the long line or the ones approaching have company logos, lettering, or signs painted on them. Every truck is anonymous, so I can't tell to whom they belong or what they carry. It can't be a coincidence that none of them are marked, though some have New Mexico and Texas license plates, while others carry Chihuahua, Mexico, plates.

These trucks remind me of the black helicopters on the *X Files* television series. Once you realize "the truth is out there," you can't help but spot them on the highways. There is no way to keep an accurate count of how many of these highly visible, yet invisible, trucks carry millions of gallons of toxic chemicals from American plants and maquiladoras (U.S.-owned factories in Mexico) across the border in Juárez. It is a silent operation that runs unimpeded. Since these diesel trucks and rigs blend into normal business traffic, no one will stop them to find out what time bombs are riding in the back. Despite laws regulating these border factories, hazardous waste gets dumped on the border every day.

These trucks have appeared at a waste facility supposedly by following designated routes marked by HC signs. They are everywhere I look in the southern New Mexico and El Paso area—white diamond-shaped highway signs with the big, green letters HC on them. Hazardous Cargo. HC signs point the way—the lawful stops, turns, and streets to get out of one area and show up with your chemical mess in another. I don't know when they first went up because they were not posted on highways and roads when I was a boy in El Paso. These warnings are a recent response to government regulations on shipping materials that have probably been sent through the area undetected and unregulated for decades. Now I spot dozens of HC signs on main streets in El Paso, by entry ramps to the freeway, and on Interstate 25 heading north toward Las Cruces. Some of the key places to find them are on the international bridges between Juárez and El Paso. If you look closely among the hundreds of cars and trucks lined up to cross each way, you will spot an HC sign.

The Southwest is the most nuclear polluted and chemically ruined area of the United States. It is the location for top-secret military installations and radioactive waste sites. Interstate 25 is the route to White Sands Missile Range, Los Alamos Nuclear Laboratory, and Cheyenne Mountain in Colorado. Secret cargoes are shipped, transferred, and secretly shifted on huge trucks every day across Arizona, New Mexico, and west Texas; I-25 is the main artery that sends government and industrial waste towards its final resting place. One of the newest dumping sites is the Waste Isolation Pilot Plant, mined 2,150 feet below an ancient salt formation thirty miles southeast of Carlsbad, New Mexico. Los Alamos National Laboratory had the honor of being the first to dump what is called "transuranic waste" at the Carlsbad site. Transuranic wastes are generated primarily during the research, development, and production of nuclear weapons. This waste includes everything from laboratory clothing, tools, glove boxes, and rubber gloves to glassware and air filters. Trucks rumbling south on I-25 and passing through El Paso carry the waste in Transuranic Packing Transporters—reusable shipping casks, three to a truck, and each filled with fifty-five-gallon steel drums of matter to be buried under the desert.

There are daily hazardous cargo caravans no one knows about; most of the people living in the area are not paying attention to the growing business of dumping dangerous materials and leftovers from a region undergoing tremendous economic and industrial changes. When state or city governments do find out, there is little they can do to stop the dangerous materials from passing through their area. The Western Governors' Association, made up of several western state governmental offices, spent ten years preparing regulations to oversee dangerous shipments, but they have not stopped the increasing tide of waste or the new companies that make money by taking care of the sludge. A landscape flooded with HC signs and thousands of trucks on the designated routes are the results of long-fought legislative and economic battles between federal and state agencies. The HC signs decorating the El Paso landscape also mean that these designated routes are here to stay, bringing the risk of chemical spills and public endangerment with them.

Hazardous waste has become big business, because the passage of NAFTA a few years ago meant more trade and more factories having to get rid of their manufacturing messes. In January 1997, Mexican President Ernesto Zedillo introduced what he called the "NAFTA Highway" to boost further trade between the United States and Mexico. He dedicated sixty-two miles of a highway running through the state of San Luis Potosí, about halfway between Mexico City and Laredo, Texas, and promised $38 million dollars to complete it. By 1998 trucks were moving 160,000 tons of products daily along the partially finished highway, about half the cargo weight now moved between the two countries in a twenty-four-hour period. When Mexico signed NAFTA, the agreement was that any dangerous materials generated by the maquiladoras must be transported back to the country of origin, even though a 1997 report by Mexico's National Institute of Ecology claimed that only 12 percent of eight million tons of hazardous wastes receive adequate treatment. Thus, more HC signs appeared all over the El Paso area along with hundreds more trucks and vans clogging the freeways. In public documents, Caldwell-Briseno estimates that 300 vehicles pass through its gates per day. Of those, 250 are commercial disposal trucks full of cargo directly from Juárez maquiladoras. These carriers dump 6,000 cubic yards per day or 1,800 tons of waste every twenty-four hours. The roads around El Paso, as well as others along the U.S.–Mexico border, are packed with heavy trucks and vans, though many local citizens might say that is just part of becoming a major city.

One encouraging step was taken in 1996 in an attempt to control these hazardous materials. The Mexican city of Nogales, on the Arizona border, conducted a Hazardous Waste Worker Training Program. They gathered one hundred Mexican workers from maquiladoras in the San Luis and Mexicali areas. The five-day program consisted of lectures on the marking, packaging, and filling out of shipping forms; placarding; and driver training. As one of the few training programs on either side of the border, it received media attention, and the Daewoo Electronics maquiladora in San Luis promised that it would increase its programs for workers and encourage other industries to do the same.

Five years later, the only media stories you hear are the ones about the increasing number of workers with medical problems caused by working conditions, the murdered Mexican girls who worked in the factories, and the growing level of contamination in the Rio Grande. In the meantime, the HC signs shake in the hot wind of a desert summer. How many truck drivers familiar with these marked routes have been trained in moving industrial waste, hydrocarbon-affected soils, and radioactive sludge? New Mexico passed a law in 1986 requiring that all hazardous waste be exported out of the state. Chances are they are not dropping it in the El Paso area because that is too close to home, so the growing number of trucks on border highways mainly come from U.S. companies producing industrial trash right across the river in Mexico.

The white diamond signs that guide these trucks to the landfill blend into the thousands of billboards, traffic lights, and highway directional signs. They have been erected to make sure the risky fallout from thriving border commerce does not wander from the plotted path and into "safe" parts of neighborhoods. The drivers must know the routes from memory by now, but as I count the HC markers, I realize the only freeway in El Paso is a legal route and so is every major street in town! I have never heard about any toxic spills in the El Paso area, yet the proliferation of the white signs on city streets and its lone freeway says the legal route is the only route. It should be evident to any El Pasoan who has noticed that the formerly sleepy town now has heavy rush hours and gridlock that a good portion of the traffic causing these problems is the long parade of diesel trucks carrying their secret cargo.

I walked around Paisano Drive and asked a few people if they knew what the HC sign down the block stood for. Not one out of the eight people I stopped knew what it meant. Five said they had never noticed the sign before; one of them, a young comedian with a smirk on his face, answered, "Doesn't that mean Hispanic Culture?" The other three thought they were directional signs to Juárez.

In 1999 an environmental group working with state officials managed to keep a radioactive waste site from being constructed in Sierra Blanca, about a hundred miles southeast of El Paso, though the fight to stop the Carlsbad site failed. The underground dump in the salt flats of southeastern New Mexico is only a few years old and is being watched and regulated by a number of state and federal agencies. The volatile issues these facilities raise come and go in the media, though the inadequate highways being used to truck NAFTA waste are starting to get some attention as more stories about dangerous breakdowns by Mexican trucks appear. One estimate claims that by the year 2010, traffic on I-25 will have increased by 88 percent.

HC. I drive the streets of my hometown in the hundred-degree heat of June looking for more signs. They start to appear as I move across town. Now the white diamonds are everywhere because I am looking for them, though normally their green letters on white are rather inconspicuous. While I drive around town counting HC signs, the radio reports that in northern New Mexico, the Los Alamos fire is out of control. It has destroyed dozens of houses and rolled over parts of the nuclear laboratory compound. Government officials claim there is no danger of the fire reaching concrete-covered storage sites. I drive the streets of El Paso and find what I have been looking for in the furnace of the afternoon.

I am back on Paisano, one of the streets closest to the Rio Grande channel and a quick route to Caldwell-Briseno, a few miles away. There are two HC signs near the last exit before downtown El Paso. Both are spray-painted in graffiti, the only defaced ones I have found all day. The first diamond glows in orange letters that turn the HC into AO, perhaps an attempt to abbreviate "asshole." The second is more creative. Someone has used black paint to change the green H into two black crosses, † †, and the O into a black peace sign, ☮. I had no idea today's taggers knew that symbol. At the red traffic light, my car waits in the middle of a three-lane side road leading to the freeway. The lanes on either side of me are filled by several diesel rigs, their long, sleek bodies humming quietly as their drivers wait for the light to change, black smoke from their exhaust pipes swirling toward the blue sky of a busy, working day.

The Border Is Closed

There is no space wider than that of grief. :: Pablo Neruda

I am turned away at Aguirre Springs and stop the car on the two-lane highway leading to the park on the east side of the Organ Mountains. High peaks and sheer red cliffs make my heart pound with anxiety. I have not been to this favorite spot of mine in twenty-two years and can't get any closer to the dominating presence of these mountains I climbed decades ago. I need to turn around; my breath is getting short, and the sheer force of finding myself alone in the desert is tearing apart my desire to enter the isolated canyon and retrace high trails to the waterfall at the top. This has never happened before. I have never been afraid to explore remote areas of the desert. Have I been gone that long? The wide fields of yucca and the narrow arroyos push me away. Sunlight flashes across the Organs to alight on top of them, and the knife shape of their jagged peaks makes me turn the car around on the narrow road and drive away.

In Laredo, Texas, thousands of Mexican Americans celebrate George Washington's birthday. An annual parade is the highlight of a sixteen-day festival in which boys and girls dress up as the first president and his wife, Martha, their white wigs glistening in the Texas sun as the procession of Spanish-speaking, brown-skinned patriots marches down the cracked asphalt streets. A series of floats features the Martha Washington Society debutantes wearing handmade colonial velvet and satin gowns that cost from $15,000 to $25,000. The society's founders were mostly Anglo women, but today's members and debutantes come from wealthy Mexican American families. City officials say they are proud to be Americans and have chosen Washington to symbolize the freedom they enjoy as Mexican American citizens of a great country. They are so proud that the year 2000 parade featured Border Patrol officers waving to the friendly crowd from their green cruisers.

I walk from my hotel in Phoenix to search for a café to have breakfast, as the place where I'm staying is isolated from the business district by a freeway overpass leading to the airport. I pass on the McDonald's at the corner and wait for the light to change so I can cross to a shopping mall across the wide boulevard. Phoenix leads the nation in pedestrian deaths caused by motorists not stopping at red lights, so I carefully step into the street when the light changes. As I cross, a group of at least twenty Mexican laborers watches me from the McDonald's lot. None of them is eating. When I get to the other side and wait for the next light, a rusting pickup screeches into the lot, the long-haired and bearded Anglo driver waving to the Mexicans to get out of the way. The tiny vehicle rocks back and forth as seven or eight men fight to jump into the back. The truck quickly sputters away as three more laborers hang on to the back gate, two of them jumping off and one making it on board. The unlucky ones return to the men who didn't try to get onto the truck this time. In the morning light I see four more groups, totaling thirty-two Mexicans, at the corners of this busy intersection. Some sit on the sidewalk, while others stand and talk to each other. They are "illegal aliens" searching for work, and the McDonald's is a designated place to wait for people to swing by and grab laborers needed for a job. Some men fight to get taken, and others acknowledge the unspoken etiquette of first come, first served. When I return from my breakfast, many are still waiting, their dirty clothes, sweat-stained caps, and defeated looks welcoming me to Phoenix.

I ask a clerk in the crowded shop in Santa Fe to name some best-selling items tourists from around the world buy from her. After pointing out a few earrings and a heavy turquoise bracelet priced at $1,200, she tells me "the bag of Indian toys" is very popular. "Indian toys?" I ask. "Yes, we just got a new shipment because they keep selling out." She leads me to a huge basket. Inside each bag, a feathered war bonnet is wrapped around a small toy cardboard-and-plastic drum to which a pair of tom-toms is attached. The cartoon on each bag shows Indian children dancing around a fire, their long bonnets flying in the air behind them, their hands raised to their mouths as they holler around the flames, preparing for a mighty battle. I walk out, and two doors down I pass a wooden sign swaying in the cold wind above another glassed-in shop: Art on the Warpath Gallery.

The crowd in the Smithsonian Museum of American History in Washington, D.C., stays away from the New Mexico Encounters exhibit, preferring the impressive showrooms on the history of the automobile or the neat covered wagons that rumbled across the west. I am the only one in the New Mexico room. A conversation I overheard on the subway to the Smithsonian explains why this exhibit is ostracized by the public. A young D.C. couple tells visiting, out-of-town friends to stay away from the American History exhibits because, as the woman says, "They've been taken over by the genocide groups. Those political groups are saying everybody was killed. It's too political. Don't go to the New Mexico show they just put up." That is exactly where I am going, so I keep listening. "Yeah," her husband tells his friends, "genocide has taken over. We can't take the kids there, so we take them to see the dinosaurs at the natural history place." Huge black-and-white photos of Reyes Tijerina's 1960s' takeover of federal land in northern New Mexico highlight the exhibit. Other panels show the Spanish conquest of the pueblos, civil rights struggles in Albuquerque, and other land grant battles—not the typical view of the Land of Enchantment. Who allowed such a politically oriented exhibit, I wonder, as I stroll through the empty rooms. Then it hits me. The tone of this presentation will certainly turn many tourists away, but something is missing. Where is New Mexico's love-hate relationship with the atomic bomb?

I drive south from Santa Fe toward the spreading metropolis of Albuquerque. Interstate 35 is jammed with cars; the section between the two cities is notorious for traffic jams and accidents. I move at thirty-five miles an hour; diesel trucks and motor homes pass me or impede my progress. Billboard after billboard greets tourists' eyes and helps me fight the boredom of a congested highway: "Jackalope Trading. Pottery. Rugs. Indian Blankets. Genuine Pueblo Jewelry." Suddenly, on the left side of the highway, a huge sign breaks the monotony. "New Mexico. #1 in Nuclear Weapons. #1 in Poverty. Coincidence?" I can't believe it. No individual or organizational name appears on the colorful billboard; whoever paid to hang this message over the desert plains leading into the largest city in the state preferred to remain anonymous. I wish I could see the sign behind again, but I can't slow down because I am being tailgated by a huge truck. I want to reread the words "Nuclear Weapons"—a phrase you rarely hear in New Mexico. I come to a long hill on the highway, right before one of my favorite places, San Felipe Pueblo. Its ancient adobe houses and historic role in the Pueblo Indian Revolt of 1690 have drawn me to visit before. I reach the crest, expecting to see the familiar green sign to the turnoff and the pueblo in the distance. I almost brake at what greets me instead. An electric billboard reveals progress: "San Felipe Casino. Gambling. Fun for the Whole Family. Games. Prizes. Food." Behind the glittering sign is the new sand-colored building about the size of four or five Wal-Marts. At ten in the morning, the parking lot is full. San Felipe Casino was built sometime between my last visit, five years ago, and this passage under the flashing billboard. This magnetic sign is enormous compared to the nuclear weapons billboard. Its pulsing electricity sets off the kind of explosions tourists are drawn to, towering lights forming the perfect combination of words and invitations that flash a monetary language over the desert. An open stretch of highway carries me beyond the palace alone, because the parade of vehicles exits at the casino. A few miles past San Felipe, on the outskirts of Albuquerque, I am greeted by two billboards that complete this visual journey across the desert. At one of the first city exits, a huge blowup of a happy woman and her three kids smiles down on traffic. The billboard announces, "Mother Murdered East of Placitas. For Reward Call 505-421-8922." I swallow but don't have time to ponder the family portrait made public because the next exit is decorated with the last sign I note before finding my hotel: "Nuclear Weapons Are Incompatible with the Peace We Seek in the 21st Century." No mushroom clouds, only fancy lettering that resembles a Christmas card greeting.

I am nervous about stepping inside, having gone through a driver's license and car registration check at the armed sentry gate of Kirkland Air Force base in Albuquerque. The B-52 bomber parked in the lot greets me with its wide, sky-blue wings, the old thing looking brittle in the January cold but doing its duty in drawing visitors to the National Atomic Museum. It is a replica of the *Enola Gay,* the plane that dropped the atomic bomb on Hiroshima in 1945. The museum lobby is devoted to Pierre and Marie Curie, discoverers of uranium and winners of Nobel Prizes in 1903. Documentary panels and photographs of the Curie family and laboratory fill three walls, celebrating the couple's greatness and showing how their lifetime commitment to uranium brought the human race into a modern world. Marie won a second Nobel in 1911. One of the largest photos is of her posing with Albert Einstein in 1925. The story of the uranium pioneers in the lobby doesn't mention that she died in 1934 from radiation poisoning after years of accumulating it in her body or that Pierre died years before, the danger of his obsession realized at an early age. The elderly volunteer at the counter shows me a map of the museum and points out that a film on Hiroshima will be shown in half an hour in a tiny room with video monitors. I pass the room as I enter the main exhibit area, where a sign above the door says History Mystery Theatre. It is located across from the gift shop, which dominates the entrance. I delay going in to the shop to find out what kinds of atomic goodies are sold, but I can't help noticing the racks of T-shirts with Einstein's face and the ones that set the tone for the place—T-shirts with either black-and-white or color images of the Trinity mushroom cloud! Take your pick. To the left of the gift shop, a mannequin of a woman lies on a hospital bed, covered in sheets. The operating room is dominated by a huge neon sign that blinks: "The Progress of Nuclear Medicine." This latest stage of our atomic tale is clearly separated from the rooms that tell the bigger story. Above the first exhibit that really begins the tour hangs the sign that says it all—"Waging Peace: The Challenge of Nuclear Stewardship." A sculpture of a sword in stone, along with a Greek waving another sword, is encased in glass. The narrative under Waging Peace reads, "You are entering the history of the most awesome instruments of destruction ever conceived." This blunt sign is in contrast with another exhibit I saw at the Albuquerque Art Museum two summers ago. I bypassed familiar sections on the destruction of the pueblos and the coming of the Spanish to focus on Albuquerque in the early 1950s. What drew me to the wall panels was a poster drawing of a young boy applauding an atomic bomb, a logo used in the public schools in 1952. Stickers and flyers with this proud image flooded classrooms when representatives from the military talked to students about the wonders of the atomic bomb. Many of the children were already familiar with the caricature because the Atomic Energy Commission had its "Atomic Float" participate in Albuquerque's annual parade. A massive black-and-white photo showed a crowd lining a downtown street and waving to the young girls riding atop a mock nuclear reactor and bomb, smoke coming out of the weapon, the whole thing dressed up in what looked like flowers and bright streamers. Alongside the school poster and parade photo was a flyer on how to build a bomb shelter and protect yourself against nuclear attack. Several shots of proud citizens digging in their desert backyards illustrated the instructions.

Now, as I enter the first section of the Atomic Museum, I wonder if I will see copies of the logo, with the young boy loving the bomb. The introductory corridor, called the Road to Manhattan, is lined with portraits of Greek philosophers and bits of their wisdom. I don't want to read about Aristotle, so I turn to something that looks out of place here. "Medieval Arms Control" reads the label above a glass case containing a crossbow and arrows. Next to it, an enormous mural of a World War I battle scene dominates the wall. I stand back and gaze at the intricate painting of dozens of U.S. doughboys lying dead in trenches, crawling out of them, and being led away by fellow soldiers after being gassed by the Germans. The distracting sign above, which says "Dawn of Modern Arms Control," is repeated on a small card on the glass cube that encloses an antique gas mask and an army helmet. Behind me, a boy and his father, the only visitors besides me, talk quietly in front of a black-and-white photograph of Albert Einstein. They wander off when the boy spots the missiles in the next room. I take their place before a blowup of a letter from Einstein to Franklin D. Roosevelt dated August 2, 1939. Einstein states his concerns to FDR about the "power of uranium and our recent progress with fission." Near the end of the letter, he expresses optimism that the wisdom and leadership of FDR will lead the United States to find good uses for these discoveries. The whole wall is devoted to Einstein, whose wild hair and large moustache is the most duplicated image in the entire building, even more than Marie Curie or mushroom clouds.

Einstein's somber photos are strategically placed to lead visitors into the main part of the museum, titled "Trinity: The Birth of an Age." A huge and colorful blowup of Trinity's mushroom cloud, the first atomic explosion, is mounted alongside a gallery of Los Alamos scientists, whose portraits are dominated by Robert Oppenheimer's. To make sure I know that the 1945 test explosion, detonated 150 miles north of El Paso, was a turning point in history, the Trinity mushroom cloud is repeated all over the room in black and white and in color. Its red-and-yellow pillar of fire rises off the desert floor, greeting you as the first image you see when you turn the corner. Another enormous photo, this one of the Trinity crater, hangs alongside the black-and-white explosion. One of the main goals of the material in this room is to convince us the secret work on the atomic bomb at Los Alamos was normal. Several glass cases hold cooking pots, eating utensils, an old phonograph, a chess board, children's toys, and other domestic evidence of the daily lives of the scientists and their families, who were secluded for years at the labs. I study the knives, forks, and ice skates, then turn to my right where the mushroom clouds rise into the darkness. Am I supposed to connect the eating utensils with the explosion?

Perhaps the next massive sign will tell me. "The Decision to Drop: Who Would Be First?" summarizes the hard decisions American leaders had to make. Which Japanese city should be disintegrated first? I don't want to read about Hiroshima or Nagasaki, can't face it because of what I have already seen and the language chosen to present what happened. I am only halfway through the building and already know what the narratives, signs, and captions under the displays of mass destruction are going to say, what point of view they are taking to make sure there is no wavering over the reasons for this museum. I glance briefly at the remains of Hiroshima and Nagasaki—image after image of blackened ruins and miles of leveled city blocks. In this carefully planned and manipulative place, there is one thing missing that I would expect to see here—images of the human destruction, evidence of what the atomic bombs did to the human body. Where are the graphic shots of the Japanese survivors or the charred remains of bodies? As gruesome as they might be, they are not part of this story. The earlier mural of the American doughboys being gassed is the only image of direct human agony in the entire museum. In offering this atomic history to its citizens, the U.S. government has made sure the human side is not in focus, except for professionally posed and photographed portraits of Oppenheimer and his crew of scientists, wearing coats and tie and big smiles—profiles of men most Americans can't identify. Despite their neat appearances throughout the place, these men are dwarfed by bombs, missiles, and the technologically evolved killing machines that completed the job first processed in their minds and their notebook calculations.

I feel queasy when I reach the core of the museum, the replicas of Fat Man and Little Boy, the bombs dropped on Hiroshima and Nagasaki that ended World War II. They lie on heavy steel carriages, Fat Man a huge bomb painted yellow and looking like a sausage or mutated lemon. Little Boy is small and sleek, its navy-blue fins shining beyond the dull gray walls of the room. The history of their creation and every possible scientific blue print for how they were assembled line the walls, along with a fascinating picture of an enormous hoist whose yards of chain are wrapped around the test bomb exploded at Trinity. One of the main reasons I came here was to see these bombs, but the brightly colored replicas push me onward, the sleek and modern paint on their forms a dressed-up attempt to soothe the eye and make them less scary. The final item that makes me pause is a model of a Norden bombsight, the same kind used by the gunner on the *Enola Gay*. At first glance, it looks like an antique microscope. Hovering over the glass case, I can barely look through the dark eyesight, and I wonder how the bombardier was able to focus through the lens and release the bomb at the exact moment he was trained to do. The labels explain this kind of eyesight was used in the war in Vietnam until 1968. I want to see what the bombardier saw and strain to line up my eye over the hole, the top of the glass case obstructing my view. I hear other museum guests shuffling behind me as they enter the room. Then I ask myself, "What am I doing? Why do I want to look through the bombsight?" I hang back in a daze, readjust my eyeglasses, and take a final look at Fat Man and Little Boy. The blue and yellow bombs shine quietly, so magnetic and repelling at the same time; I want to touch them. There are no sensors or signs telling me to keep my hands away, but I can't make myself do it. I can't touch Fat Man or Little Boy, though their cold hearts beg for human contact. Suddenly the father and son I saw earlier appear next to me and I hear the child whispering something to his dad. The man nods and the little boy rubs the shimmering yellow steel of Fat Man. I move away and hurry into the next room.

The Cold War exhibit contains too many missiles and weapons of mass destruction to list. Some of them sound familiar—the Titan missiles and U2 spy planes—but the bombs I have never seen before are frightening in the way the museum curators have set them up. Is there such a thing as a "curator" of atomic weapons? Early fission bombs are mounted alongside MK8 and BOAR atomic rockets. The ugliest ones are the three-foot-tall nuclear shells that stand in a row, their green metal skins surrounding a huge photo of soldiers loading a shell into a howitzer. In the 1950s, the army was prepared to fire these shells during a ground battle. Several nuclear torpedoes from submarines of the era are mounted vertically to form a fence around the MK39 hydrogen bomb, the type that has never been dropped on humanity, though several were detonated during tests in the Pacific fifty years ago. At this point, the technology of destruction accelerates; the abundant samples of Cold War weapons blend into the 1960s' exhibit. Displays of newer missiles focus on spy satellites and devices to detect nuclear detonations around the world. These are followed by a rather tame presentation on the Cuban missile crisis of 1962. Not much is revealed about how close the world came to annihilation as John F. Kennedy and Nikita Khrushchev played their nuclear game with Fidel Castro and his island.

The closing exhibits compress the last thirty years of nuclear history into a small space, as models of weapons are replaced by the kind of overblown slogans I found earlier. "U.S. National Security Objectives" are listed as part of the grand finale—a comment on the state of the world after the United States and the forces of good have won the nuclear race. Responsibility, knowledge, and strength dominate these last panels, which present the ultimate specimen of triumph—pieces of the Berlin Wall piled inside another glass case. I stare at the old bricks and shards of mortar, the mess lying under a color photo of Germans celebrating the tearing down of the wall. Ronald Reagan's speech—"Mr. Gorbachev, tear down that wall!"—is quoted several times. I have gone from Greek philosophers to crossbows and gas masks to old phonograph players preceding Fat Man and Little Boy. I have moved from Einstein's warning letter to attractive portraits of Robert Oppenheimer and the glaring absence of images of the dead at Hiroshima. I have gone this far to end with a pile of bricks! Are these the supreme ruins of triumphant democracy? Is this what it comes down to—bricks and mortar torn apart by human hands? Or could they represent the remains of civilization pulverized by a push of a button? This is our nuclear history, our death cult, a triumph over evil through our skillful controlling of our own power. Bricks and mortar ripped apart to teach the world a lesson. I shake my head and wonder if the curators will ever add a burned piece of wood from a house in Hiroshima. There is no one else in this last hallway, where the door leads outside to another B-52 bomber like the *Enola Gay*, its wings welcoming guests to marvel at how we delivered the prize. I shake my head again and want to write something in the pocket notebook I carry, but all I can do is gaze at the remains of the Berlin Wall. This is it. The sign opening the exhibit flashes across my mind—"You are entering the history of the most awesome instruments of destruction ever conceived." I mumble the phrase to myself and wish I could hold one of those bricks in my hand. Each brick not only contains the story of the Cold War, but is made from the same grains of sand as White Sands National Monument, where Trinity was molded and exploded over the same desert where I grew up. It is taken apart by the same hands that re-create and revise history to make sure we know how powerful we are and how we will dictate the future survival of mankind. I think of my Southwest with its deserts and mountains, its struggling and polluted Rio Grande. Most of all, these bricks are torn apart in the same ways millions of people tear the border apart, the United States and Mexico wrestling with their own Berlin Wall. It is no coincidence Trinity was exploded in New Mexico. This was the chosen place because timeless forces of great conflict have used the desert as their stage for hundreds of years. Its landscape of beauty and killing power is the terrain of bloody history. From the Anasazi to the Spanish to Oppenheimer and the youngest Border Patrol recruit—they all must have knelt in the desert, sooner or later, and grabbed a handful of sand to form it into bricks for cliff houses, churches of unquestionable faith, or bunkers to house splitting atoms. Brick upon brick in the desert heat, where even the remains of the Berlin Wall will disintegrate someday. I can't comprehend why this museum takes visitors from crossbows and murals of doughboys in agony to a pile of bricks. Fat Man and Little Boy stand in the way of that course. Most New Mexicans aren't aware of this story or its proximity to them. When it comes to the atomic bomb, they have behaved like most Americans, accepting what can't be understood because the forces of democracy say it is safe not to understand. All they want is total victory at any price. This museum with its bricks of farewell proves the whole story is no longer an eternal struggle between good and evil. One side has already won, and the many weapons in this building keep me from completely seeing where the sun is shining when I exit the museum.

I can't ponder this stuff anymore because the bricks were the last thing I expected after being bombarded with the evolution of mass killing and its brilliant instruments, a lethal technology described here by manipulated narratives of victory. I walk quietly toward the exit and almost bump into the next two visitors, a young Japanese couple who smile politely at me as I move aside to let them enter.

Waiting to see a movie in an Albuquerque shopping mall, I lick my ice cream cone and lean back on an uncomfortable bench, the images of the previous day's immersion in atomic history slowly fading. It is early afternoon on a weekday and a few people linger around the food court by the theaters. Several of them come out as their movie ends, including a middle-aged Chicano man. He holds a hardcover book under his arm, and his white goatee, black beret, and sunglasses seem out of place. He wears an expensive-looking leather jacket and his hair under the beret is neatly combed. Did he watch his movie with the shades on? As he sits on a bench across from me, I read the marquee. One of the titles catches my eye. "Vampire" is showing. I look at the letters above me, lick my ice cream, then turn to the man again. He has eased himself back on the bench and opened his book. I can see the cover clearly. It is a novel by Anne Rice on vampires. I finish my cone and buy my admission ticket to one of the other movies that I was planning to see.

The American International Rattlesnake Museum is located in the middle of Old Town in Albuquerque, a popular tourist area preserved in the Spanish colonial style. The snake zoo, as people call it, is hidden in the back of the shop, rows of glass aquariums containing more than twenty species of rattlesnakes. After paying my $2.50 fee and walking past shelves overflowing with rattlesnake baseball caps, coffee cups, T-shirts, decals, key chains, and, of course, rubber snakes, I hesitate before the swinging doors into the exhibit.

A fat and beautiful gila monster lizard sleeps in the first aquarium, the dull pink and black spots on its body hiding lethal power. The sign on the glass says that Mollie the Gila Monster is tame and is one of the oldest residents of the place. The reptile doesn't move or open its eyes as I tiptoe by. I pause cautiously as tiger and Mojave rattlers move their tiny heads, then go back to sleep. Their passive demeanor is in sharp contrast to the desert massasauga, a small and aggressive rattler that snaps to attention and follows me with its piercing eyes. Its black skin is luminescent, its desire to strike reflected by the dull tap of its nose against the glass. We stare at each other, goose bumps running up and down my arms. I think it would strike if it could. There is a second room of snakes, but I can't proceed because another snake as alert as the massasauga waits at the entrance. It is a huge eastern diamondback curled in a tree inside a glass cage. It moves its heavy body and follows me with shiny, black eyes. It is at least five feet long and acts like it wants to fly out of the tree and lunge at me. This massive snake swings part of its thick body off the tree but doesn't fall. Like an acrobat, it balances on thin branches and waits without taking its eyes off me.

The next room holds every reptile imaginable, from western pygmy and timber rattlers to a Costa Rican snake, plus a rare Vrocoan rattler from Venezuela that is hanging in a tree. There is even a beautiful albino rattler whose skin is more tan than white, another set of disturbing black eyes making the point these snakes are all embedding into my memory. They are reptiles in captivity, but the energy and the possibilities hang electric in the air of the musty and dark room. I find a small monitor lizard and two green iguanas sleeping inside their cages. Actually, most of these creatures are asleep except for the Vrocoan and the timber. I always had the notion rattlers from northern climates would be more passive, but the timber surprises me by appearing to be the meanest, its small head giving off a sense of evil and a demeanor more threatening than the diamondbacks.

I sense something at my back and turn to the six-foot western diamondback skin hanging on the wall, its flat length longer than my body, its intricate markings beautiful and undecipherable. Next to it, in the smallest aquarium in the place, is a Venezuelan green bottle blue tarantula—an ugly spider busy weaving its nest through a wire screen and twigs. I watch the tarantula and hear a scratching behind me. I need to leave and quickly pass the eastern diamondback; more than half its body hangs in midair as if suspended by magic. As I go to the front of the shop, the enormous snake slithers out of the tree and vanishes into the leaves lining its cage. I hear a sound from years ago—the canyon opening at Cottonwood Springs allows midmorning sunlight to splash off dead tree trunks to reveal the biggest rattlesnake a boy in the desert has ever seen, its coiled fortress of a body waiting for me to get closer. I am handed a decal by the woman behind the counter as I leave. Able to breathe freely again outside, I examine the sticker: "American International Rattlesnake Museum. I Survived."

"Here I sit, buns a flexin', giving birth to another Texan"—graffiti on the wall of a toilet stall in the bathroom of a restaurant in Old Town.

A sample of book titles taken from the "Hispanic" sections in several Barnes and Noble and Borders bookstores in Albuquerque:

How Did You Get to Be Mexican?
There's a Word for It in New Mexico
Something to Declare
Anything but Mexican
Occupied America
Working in the Dark
Latino Heretics

From Bamba to Hip Hop

Speaking Chicana

Nuevo México Profundo

Dangerous Border Crossers

Muy Macho

Life Is Hard

Thirty Million Strong

Platicas de Mi Barrio

Son of Two Bloods

Guide to the Perfect Latin American Idiot

My Bloody Life

Jose, Can You See?

Canto, Grito y Mi Liberación

Hispanics in Hollywood

A Patriot after All

Ethnic Labels, Latino Lives

Latinos Unidos

Cantinflas and the Chaos of Mexican Modernity

Hating Whitey

Images of Penance, Images of Mercy

Cholos y Surfers

In Search of Respect: Selling Crack in the Barrio

Hombres y Machos

The Latino Holiday Book

Going Down to the Barrio

Gringo Justice

Born in Blood and Fire

The following passage is from an article by Annick Treuger on Chicano murals, taken from an *Encyclopedia Brittanica* entry on the U.S.–Mexico border.

From the *UNESCO Courier,* March 1, 1999. Section: World of Painting:

Chicanos Paint Their Way Back
In Arizona, Texas, California, and New Mexico, Chicanos (Mexican immigrants and/or their descendents) are sizeable minorities which are still growing as a result of immigration. It is hard for them to get

a foothold in American society and many of them live in barrios (Spanish for neighborhoods), either in the center of big cities or on their outskirts, away from areas where there are jobs. These communities tend to be self-contained and generate self-destructive tensions and conflicts. Young Chicanos face many problems—dropping out of school, violent gang rivalry, alcoholism, drug dealing, and illegal gun possession—all of which can lead to serious gang warfare stirred up by agents of organized crime.

What is wrong with the previous paragraph? I want to deconstruct some of Treuger's key statements:

"sizeable minorities which are still growing as a result of immigration." She must be saying the brown hordes are invading the border and over-populating barrios. Could this influence an anti-immigration, "Let's close the border and arm ourselves" kind of mentality?

"It is hard for them to get a foothold in American society." They are Chicano, many are illegal, and they live in barrios on the other side of the railroad tracks, so they can't get with it. Most don't speak English, so they can't get a foothold. Run for it!

"many of them live in barrios." A typographical error? Did her original draft say "They all live in barrios," those evil nests of brown bees spreading toward our suburban lawns? In the encyclopedia, *barrio* is a dirty word.

"away from areas where there are jobs." She says there are no jobs in neighborhoods. Period. No jobs where people live. The brown hordes flock together, unlike other social groups, and live far from job sites. A normal American always lives where there are jobs.

"generate self-destructive tensions and conflicts." Pregnant teenage Chicanas, the single-parent home, father in prison, the gang bangers, thousands of illegal aliens washing dishes at greasy cafés. How can they not generate self-destructive tensions and conflicts? Unlike the normal American family, they are caught in vicious cycles of self-destruction.

"drug dealing and illegal gun possession." How about inviting the National Rifle Association to open chapters in barrios? Their membership would swell by millions. As for dealing dope, how about sending several thousand more marines to Colombia, South America?

And the standout phrase: "gang warfare stirred up by agents of organized crime." Who are these agents of organized crime? It can't be the gang boys who are too busy generating self-destructive tensions and conflicts. No organization there. It can't be adult Chicano males who are all in prison. Who are these agents stirring up warfare in the dark barrios of America? Chinese spies tired of stealing atomic secrets from Los Alamos? Leftover Soviet saboteurs from the Cold War? Could it be Jerry Falwell and his followers, checking out new real estate they can purchase after the barrio is torn down? How many agents of organized crime did Treuger interview, and how did she identify them when hundreds of homeboys are hanging out on barrio street corners, keeping their stoned, cold eyes on this writer as she tries to gather data for her article? Isn't UNESCO a United Nations organization?

From the June 5, 1900, *El Paso Herald,* published twelve years before the Mexican Revolution, one of the most catastrophic events in twentieth-century North American history that cost the lives of more than 250,000 Mexicans:

Our sister republic of Mexico stands upon the threshold of the dawning century with wonderful social, political, and industrial development to its credit. The introduction of railways, the infusion of modern business methods, the widening of industrial effort, and the adjustment of laws and education to new opportunity have constituted the potential agents of Mexico's advancement within the past 15 years of its most conspicuous progress. During this period, Mexico has increased its number of consular representatives in foreign countries from 107 to 208. This fact tells the story of Mexico's progress in establishing commercial relations with countries beyond its borders. Within 15 years, Mexican imports have increased in volume to the extent of $28,000,000 gold per year, and exports have more than tripled. The value of coffee exported has grown from a million and a half to eight million per year. The tobacco now exported, amounting to upward of four million pounds a year, forms a business that has been created in recent years. The value of cattle exported each year has increased to four and a half million. Increasing trade has been responsible for the establishment of fourteen new and branch banks. To all this must be added the increase in primary schools, which after all, is the basic strength of the republic. These schools have grown in number from 5,560 in 1884 to 9,593 in 1900. Mexico is traveling in leaps and bounds to the rank of a first world power.

From the Associated Press, June 4, 2000:

Four days into what she was told would be a six-hour trip, Yolanda Gonzalez lay dead of dehydration in the southern Arizona desert—a victim of the 110-degree heat. Gonzalez was one of six undocumented immigrants to have died of heat-related exposure in the past week in the Arizona desert. She was one of nineteen to die since last October. Heat-related deaths are an annual occurrence on this parched section of the border, which draws those immigrants who don't believe they can get into the United States anywhere else. But they're more of a concern this year, when immigrants are pouring into the state by the thousands each month. Federal authorities have met the surge with increased enforcement, which in turn is pushing more crossers to try remote and forbidden stretches of rugged terrain.

Sign at a Border Patrol checkpoint east of El Paso, June 2000: "Illegal crossers sent back to date this year: 7,562."

From the Associated Press, June 6, 2000:

In a new instance of border friction, a Mexican activist Monday offered $10,000 to anybody who kills a U.S. Border Patrol agent. Carlos Ibarra Perez, sixty, says too many undocumented immigrants are being slain by federal agents and private landowners while making their way into the United States, and he wants to avenge their deaths. "They (the Border Patrol) are massacring people," said Ibarra, spokesman for a seven-thousand-member advocacy group called the Citizen Defense Committee. "And now we're ready to defend ourselves." Incensed U.S. officials immediately opened an investigation into Ibarra's threat and FBI agents were expected to review a videotape of Ibarra's news conference. Mounting tensions between undocumented immigrants, federal authorities, and border residents has been evident. Two weeks ago, a Border Patrol agent in Brownsville shot and killed an undocumented immigrant during a morning struggle on the banks of the Rio Grande. In Arizona, ranchers are fighting back against what they call "a literal invasion of illegal immigrants." Some patrol property from towers armed with rifles. A state attorney general's office in Mexico City said it has opened a criminal investigation of Ibarra. "The man is inciting violence. This could lead to an international incident," spokesman Ruben Dario said from the state attorney general's office.

Billboard on East Montana Avenue, El Paso, summer 2000: "Border Patrol Agents Wanted. Good Jobs. Good Benefits. Call 831-4972."

The latest news from Arizona: A group that calls itself the "American Way Team" has been distributing thousands of flyers all over the border inviting people "to hunt down undocumented Mexicans."

From the *El Paso Times,* June 1, 2001:

Mexican President Vicente Fox caused quite a stir among U.S. government officials when he announced the Mexican government would provide survival kits to any Mexican citizen attempting to cross the border into the United States. These kits would contain bottled water, food, and medical supplies. This announcement comes after seven Mexicans were found dead in the Arizona desert last week, all of them illegals attempting to cross in the 120-degree heat. This brings the total number of deaths by Mexicans in the desert to thirty-two for the year. After an exchange of messages between the Bush administration and the Mexican government,

President Fox said he would issue another statement regarding the survival kits and his administration's reconsideration of manufacturing such kits.

The sign on the entrance to the Border Patrol Museum in El Paso reads "Firearms Prohibited." Before I can touch the door, a tall man with rough cowboy features swings it open. He mumbles "Welcome" and steps aside. I enter the air-conditioned building that looks like a former warehouse. Like other museums I have visited recently, I am the only guest. The man is the lone attendant and returns to his work behind a glass counter containing Border Patrol flags, banners, watches, patches, sunglasses, binoculars, and other tools. At one end is a row of rotating hangers weighed down with Border Patrol T-shirts, jackets, sweatshirts, and other clothing, every item for sale. The clerk stands at the counter, both hands on the glass, and watches me. The fact that the U.S. government has the nerve to create a Border Patrol museum in one of the most volatile regions of the border makes me nervous, but an exhibit titled *Illegal Substances* draws my attention. The glass case is full of pot pipes, roach clips, and other smoking devices confiscated by Border Patrol agents. Next to the paraphernalia, a gas tank with a false compartment for drugs sits in the case like a rusting marshmallow. The narrative on the exhibit wall recounts the government's version of the war on drugs. The information focuses on the history of traffic checkpoints and how to inspect an automobile effectively for illegal substances. A black-and-white photograph from 1927 shows agents shaking down a Model T Ford at the International Bridge between Juárez and El Paso. Back then, the Texas Rangers were the prime law enforcement agency on the border and several photographs of their exploits on horseback surround the bongs and pipes. I search for photographs I've seen in books of rangers lynching Mexicans, but none are in sight.

The drug exhibit pales in comparison to the enormous cases of confiscated weapons mounted or leaning against the walls. Pistols of every type and caliber, along with knives, shears, machetes, stilettos, brass knuckles, and steel stars are everywhere. The signs describe where they were confiscated and how Border Patrol agents take weapons away from not only drug runners, but also illegal aliens. The fight against foreign populations is emphasized by the next set of cabinets. In comparison to the haphazard arrangement of the bad guns, the newer-looking compartments hold the government arsenal—shotguns, riot guns, automatic rifles, and pistols, all lined in rows as if they had just been cleaned and oiled. The contrast is highlighted with a sign above the guns—"Awareness Is Survival."

I notice movement behind me as the clerk spins a rack of Border Patrol T-shirts, dust rag in hand. He looks in my direction as he wipes the front counter, having spotted the tiny notebook and pen in my hands. I duck behind an enormous motorboat, painted in typical Border Patrol lime green, its engine glistening brighter than the guns. Next to it is a rusting smuggler's boat, its sides caved in, and a narrative describing how difficult it is for criminals to outrun government boats. Yet not all hope is lost for crossing the water without permission. A third boat in worse shape than the other two is labeled as one of the crafts Cuban "boat people" sailed to freedom. The fact that they were as illegal as Mexicans caught in the desert is overlooked—cheerful photographs show Coast Guard and patrol agents welcoming the survivors to the United States. An anti–Fidel Castro statement hangs above the boat. I appear on the other side of the boat room and find the man busy on the telephone behind the counter. I can't hear what he is saying and am distracted by other phones and communications equipment. Telegraphs, old radios, walkie talkies, and every kind of telephone used in the past century decorate a hallway leading to the part of the museum that truly represents what this place is all about—the art of capturing people. Visitors can trace the evolution of such skills from the ancient signal flags to electronic sensing devices now buried by the thousands from San Diego, California, to Brownsville, Texas.

The final room has to be the pride and joy of the Border Patrol. A roll call of honored officers, names and photos lining the corridor, ends where their history begins. Oddly enough, there are no photos of agents killed in the line of duty. Photos of captured illegals, including bracero workers from the fifties, fill the place. The sad and angry faces of Mexicans, most of them hunkered down near the ground or in holding cells, are always posed lower than the proud, smiling officers standing above them and saluting into the camera. A checkpoint from 1937 includes information on sign cutting, the art of tracking people in the desert. Devices to train police dogs and horses come alive in pictures of fleeing Mexicans, dogs biting Mexicans, and agents surrounding Mexicans. Sheets of statistics are pasted everywhere. Every year since the early part of the century is broken down by month, listing how many illegals were captured and sent back to Mexico. What is missing, of course, are the numbers of people who are never caught and the ones who keep crossing into the United States after being captured, time and time again. One recent year lists 8,597 individuals caught near El Paso in April. Multiply that by three to get the total who made it safely and are now part of an enormous working force in this country.

By the end of my tour, the story of the U.S. Border Patrol with its government slant would appear to be cut-and-dried, but I am startled by the last sign in the place, "Apprehension: Why Must People Flee Their Homelands?" It is printed to resemble a huge newspaper headline and is set inside a glass cabinet, making it the final word on illegal immigration. Beneath the title, a detailed document explains social, economic, and political issues in Mexico. The narrative concludes that the American Dream, coupled with poverty and ignorance, forces Mexicans to seek a new life in the United States. This conclusion stops short of blaming Mexico's history of revolutions, corrupt governments, and distrust of American institutions for the problem. The document emphasizes that U.S. laws will always be upheld despite harsh realities that force Mexicans to come north.

The clerk ends his telephone conversation as I stand before the final image that makes me leave the place. I find it on the wall under the USBP Roadrunner Helicopter parked near the exit doors. The sleek body of the machine doesn't show any wear and tear from its time in the desert as it hovers over an enormous rectangular photograph of several dozen Mexicans being led away in handcuffs. It is 1956 and the bracero worker program set up between the United States and Mexico is in full swing. Farms and ranches throughout the Southwest are employing thousands of Mexicans who have legal papers, but this photograph reminds visitors that despite attempts by the United States to help Mexico over the years, its people never learn and continue to break the law. A menacing holding pen lined with barbed wire is outlined in black on the right side of the photo. Three agents wait by the open gate as the long line of Mexicans is herded inside. Several of the captured men turn toward the camera. The flash of the night lens reflects in their startled eyes, their defeat wearing them down, though it is only temporary because they will cross the Rio Grande again, the border as fragile as this aging photograph.

There is a dead scorpion on the carpet, its flesh-colored body and tail drying into a husk. I came across it in the corner of the bedroom in my mother's house in El Paso. I have finished my visit, and the dead scorpion reminds me it is summer, the season for things that don't appear any other time of the year. The weeks of tremendous heat blaze off the asphalt streets to bring back images of things that do stay here all the time: electric fences, captured history framed and labeled to attract the curious and paying tourist, plus the desert mountains that look the same as they erode with the passing decades, their hard peaks and dry, brown slopes leading to the Rio Grande of restless populations. I bend down and gaze at the hooked tail of the dead scorpion. It was separated from the body when my mother crushed the thing with her "scorpion stick," a handy broomstick she keeps in the bedroom. Two pincers lie near the five-inch tail. I ask my mother about the scorpion she killed two days before I arrived. She has not had time to sweep it up and throw it in the trash, and she says she finds them clinging to the ceiling at night. Her summer ritual consists of turning off the lights in the bedroom, going about her business in the rest of the house, then coming back and turning on the lights again. Most nights, there is at least one scorpion on the ceiling. She takes her stick and approaches carefully, not wanting to startle the thing or have it fall into her hair. She holds the mighty stick with both hands, moves the tip slowly toward the creature and carefully crushes it into the ceiling before it can spring away. She points out the marks on the ceiling where she has killed each scorpion. I look up at the white paint and find brown stains like notches on a gun, tiny trails of death that might make good art in a Southwest museum, tracks of protection against what stings and rises out of a desert land that cannot escape its own power, whether it is as small as this disintegrating scorpion on the floor or as large as the locked buildings at Kirkland Air Force base at night. My mother explains this is the only way to kill scorpions, because if you try to catch them in a jar, or knock them off the ceiling, they are too fast and will get away. So far this summer she has killed eight scorpions, including one she found clinging to her nightgown one night when she got up to go to the bathroom. She saw it, flicked it off with her hand, and managed to step on it before it could disappear. I am amazed my mother has reached a point where she doesn't think twice about stepping on a scorpion. I ask her if she did this barefoot, since she was sleeping. "No way," she answers and reminds me to always put my shoes on the chair before going to bed each night. Never leave any clothes on the floor.

According to scientists at the Arizona State Museum, a female bark scorpion with two tails was captured near Nogales on February 27, 1997. It died on August 6 of that year, but not before giving birth to twelve babies on June 6. None of them had two tails. The scorpion was named Pepe and was capable of using both tails, which she could hold either crossed over one another or arched side by side. Pepe exhibited behavior similar to other bark scorpions, such as walking upside down under objects and holding its body very flat on the ground. Pepe was observed using the right tail to subdue a cricket, that tail being the tool of choice throughout her observed life. Pepe was found to fluoresce in ultraviolet light just as other scorpions do. The number of described scorpion species has increased dramatically since this phenomenon was discovered and used to locate scorpions at night. The Scorpion Men of Babylonian mythology were warriors and children of Tiamat, the dragon mother of the universe. Half-men and half-scorpion, they had human heads and arms and were scorpions from the waist down, with powerful tails they used in combat. Otherwise, they fought with bows and arrows that never missed. The Babylonians believed the Scorpion Men were the sacred guardians of their sun god, Shamash. They would open the gates of the Mountain of the East in the morning, so Shamash could rise in the sky, and close the gates of the Mountain of the West behind him in the evening as he descended into the underworld.

She leaves me alone in the room and I go to the dead scorpion. I have not seen a live one in years and will not have any luck this summer. The bedroom is the place in the house where the scorpions appear most often, where they hide from what I have been searching for along the fences of closed boundaries. My mother concludes her scorpions are coming in through cracks in the screens on the bay windows. A hedge of bushes and other plants lines the wall outside the window and she says they breed there and come right in.

Before I showed up, she took gray electric tape and covered the corners and edges of the windows. She has not seen a single scorpion since she did this and decides the tape will keep them out. I reach down and pick up the detached tail of the dead scorpion. I want to touch the tip, but I am hesitant. Does the tip have any poison, or does it simply work as a syringe when the scorpion strikes? I find a plastic bag from my suitcase and drop the tail into it. I will keep this as a souvenir and bring it back to Minnesota, my evidence from my time in the desert brittle and soft in my hand, yet it is the only thing from the Southwest that will disintegrate and disappear in a short time. The bag that holds this fragile tail is stuffed between fossils, copies of documents and old photographs, and pamphlets on how nuclear power will save the land—evidence that will certainly outlast the remains of the scorpion. That evening, when I call my wife to say hello and reveal the special gift I am bringing, she tells me she will move out if I bring a scorpion tail into the house. I laugh and tell her it is only a souvenir from a strange and brutal land. She thinks I am crazy to bring back a scorpion tail from a land I love and left long ago.

About the Author

RAY GONZALEZ is a poet, essayist, and editor born in El Paso, Texas. He is the author of *Circling the Tortilla Dragon: Short-Short Fictions* (Creative Arts, 2002); *The Ghost of John Wayne and Other Stories* (The University of Arizona Press, 2001); *Memory Fever* (The University of Arizona Press, 1999), a memoir about growing up in the Southwest; *Turtle Pictures* (The University of Arizona Press, 2000), which received the 2001 Minnesota Book Award for Poetry; and six other books of poetry, including *The Hawk Temple at Tierra Grande* (2002), *Cabato Sentora* (1999), and *The Heat of Arrivals* (1996), all three from BOA Editions. The latter received a 1997 PEN/Oakland Josephine Miles Book Award for Excellence in Literature.

He is the editor of twelve anthologies, most recently *Muy Macho: Latino Men Confront Their Manhood* and *Touching the Fire: Fifteen Poets of the Latino Renaissance* (both from Anchor/Doubleday Books) and *No One Out There Is Looking for Us: Prose Poems by 24 American Poets* (Tupelo Press, 2002). He has served as Poetry Editor for *The Bloomsbury Review* for twenty-two years and recently founded a poetry journal, *LUNA*.

His awards include a 2002 McKnight Loft Fellowship in Poetry, a 2000 Loft Literary Center Career Initiative Fellowship, a 1998 Fellowship in Poetry from the Illinois Arts Council, a 1993 Before Columbus Foundation American Book Award for Excellence in Editing, and a 1988 Colorado Governor's Award for Excellence in the Arts. He is an associate professor in the MFA Creative Writing Program at the University of Minnesota in Minneapolis.

Works by Ray Gonzalez

ESSAYS AND MEMOIRS
Memory Fever: A Journey Beyond El Paso del Norte

FICTION
Circling the Tortilla Dragon
The Ghost of John Wayne and Other Stories

POETRY
Apprentice to Volcanos
Cabato Sentora
From the Restless Roots
The Hawk Temple at Tierra Grande
The Heat of Arrivals
Railroad Face
Turtle Pictures
Twilights and Chants

ANTHOLOGIES
After Aztlan: Latino Poets of the Nineties
City Kite on a Wire: 38 Denver Poets
Crossing the River: Poets of the Western U.S.
Currents from the Dancing River: Contemporary Latino Fiction, Nonfiction, and Poetry
Inheritance of Light: Contemporary Poetry from Texas
Mirrors Beneath the Earth: Short Fiction by Chicano Writers
Muy Macho: Latino Men Confront Their Manhood
No One Out There Is Looking for Us: Prose Poems by 24 American Poets
Touching the Fire: Fifteen Poets of Today's Latino Renaissance
Tracks in the Snow: Essays by Colorado Poets
Under the Pomegranate Tree: The Best New Latino Erotica
Without Discovery: A Native Response to Columbus

JOURNALS
The Guadalupe Review
LUNA: A New Journal of Poetry